The CREOLE *Mutiny*

The
CREOLE
Mutiny

A TALE OF REVOLT
ABOARD A SLAVE SHIP

George Hendrick
Willene Hendrick

Ivan R. Dee

CHICAGO 2003

THE CREOLE MUTINY. Copyright © 2003 by George Hendrick and
Willene Hendrick. All rights reserved, including the right to reproduce this
book or portions thereof in any form. For information, address: Ivan R. Dee,
Publisher, 1332 North Halsted Street, Chicago 60622. Manufactured in the
United States of America and printed on acid-free paper.

Library of Congress Cataloging-in-Publication Data:
Hendrick, George.
    The Creole mutiny : a tale of revolt aboard a slave ship / George
Hendrick, Willene Hendrick.
        p. cm.
    Includes bibliographical references (p.) and index.
    ISBN 1-56663-493-8 (acid-free paper)
    1. Slave insurrections—United States—History—19th century. 2.
Mutiny—United States—History—19th century. 3. Creole (Brig) 4.
Washington, Madison. 5. Slaves—United States—Biography. I.
Hendrick, Willene, 1928– II. Title.

E447 .H45 2003
326'.0973—dc21   2002031589

To Emilie and Dennis

Acknowledgments

FOR MANY YEARS we discussed African-American literature and culture with the late Prof. Richard Barksdale and
the late Prof. Mildred Barksdale. Their knowledge of and passion for African-American studies greatly influenced this work.

We were aided by many librarians at the University of
Illinois at Urbana-Champaign, especially those in the Afro-
Americana Library and the Newspaper Library. Laura Branca
provided the photograph of her father, Theodore Ward.

Contents

The CREOLE *Mutiny*

Introduction

AN ESCAPED SLAVE who gave his name as Madison Washington had made his way to freedom in Canada. But in 1841, after a short time there, he determined to return to Virginia to rescue his wife from bondage. He failed to free her and was then captured and sold to a slave dealer who shipped him on the *Creole* from Richmond, Virginia, with at least 134 other black men and women, destined for the auction block in New Orleans. Off the northern Bahamian island of Abaco, Washington and eighteen followers, after a violent revolt, seized the ship and had the *Creole* sailed into Nassau, where all the slaves who wanted emancipation were eventually freed by the British government. For this action Britain was vilified by many officials in the United States and by large numbers of pro-slavery Southerners. Slave owners who had insured their "property" on the *Creole* sued the companies for their losses.

The outline of these events only hints at the human drama of a specific incident and the American conflict over the institution of slavery. In this story "freedom" and "love" are not abstractions but the real motivations of Madison Washington, who could not continue to live free in Canada while the woman he loved remained a slave. Much about Madison Washington's life remains unknown. We were unable to discover where he was born or where he lived in Virginia. We could not determine whether Madison Washington was his birth name, nor what his wife's name was. We do not know what specifically caused him to flee Virginia in the first place. From what we see of him in the official records, however, he appears to have been intelligent and independent-minded, and the idea of freedom must have burned in him for a long time before he actually stole away.

In this book we reconstruct the runaway world of Madison Washington using nineteenth-century and modern sources. After his attempt to free his wife failed and he was captured, he was bought by Thomas McCargo, a slave dealer, whom we describe along with his associates in the slave trade. Washington and his fellow slave passengers were being shipped on a domestic slave ship, but we show the similarities of conditions on these domestic ships and the plight of slaves shipped on international slave ships, where they suffered indiscriminate cruelty, sexual abuse, and physical deprivation.

Once the *Creole* was under way, the slaves began to plot a revolt. The government document describing the mutiny and the records of the ensuing insurance trials provide extensive evidence about the rebellion itself. Many of the whites on the *Creole* gave testimony about the revolt, but none of these men supported the slaves. Blacks were not allowed to tell their stories. Although gaps and mysteries remain in the *Creole* story, we recount as much as is known of why and how the mutiny occurred, and its consequences. It was an event with national and international ramifications.

In the diplomatic friction between the United States and Britain and in the insurance trials, the slaves' battle for freedom is rarely mentioned. But it is impossible to read through these official and legal accounts without admiring the courage of all the slaves involved, their determination to live free and to escape the oppression imposed on them by local, state, and federal governments in the United States. The *Creole* matter ends ironically with slave owners being reimbursed for the "property" they lost during the mutiny.

The slaves themselves disappear from official records. All our efforts to locate their later histories and their descendants failed. Robert Harms, in his splendid book *The Diligent: A Voyage Through the Worlds of the Slave Trade,* about the trip of a French slave ship in 1731, was similarly unable to locate the descendants of the *Diligent* slaves who landed in Martinique. Harms writes that although their names "have been forever lost to history, somewhere their descendants have survived, endured, and perhaps triumphed." We hope this same statement is true of the descendants of Madison Washington and his fellow slaves who revolted successfully to gain their freedom, and who were protected and freed by the government of Queen Victoria at a time when the United States government worked vigorously to see that they should not be free.

In an Appendix we sum up the accounts of five authors—Frederick Douglass, William Wells Brown, Lydia Maria Child, Pauline Elizabeth Hopkins, and Theodore Ward—who wrote about Madison Washington and the *Creole* mutiny. Their accounts are mostly fiction but testify to the enduring importance of the event.

Writing of slaves who revolted—including Madison Washington—Henry Highland Garnet, the black abolitionist minister, remarked in "An Address to the Slaves of the United States of America" (1843): "Noble men! Those who have fallen in freedom's conflict, their memories will be cherished by the truehearted and the God-fearing in all future generations; those who are living, their names are surrounded by a halo of glory." Madison Washington, with his desire for freedom and his wish to remove his wife from bondage, acted heroically, but his failure to rescue his wife casts him as a tragic hero.

The Crew and Passengers
on the Creole

Captain Robert Ensor, from Richmond, Virginia. Wounded in the mutiny.
First Mate Zephaniah C. Gifford, slightly wounded in the revolt.
Second Mate Lucius Stevens.

Crew:
Blinn Curtis, wounded in the mutiny.
*William Devereux, a free man of color who was cook and steward.
*Francis Foxwell.
Jacques Lacombe, a Frenchman who did not speak English. He remained at the wheel during the rebellion.
*John Silvy. He may be the sailor called "Antonio."
*Henry Speck.

Allowed to remain in the cabin:
Lewis, an old slave belonging to the slave trader Thomas McCargo. Lewis acted as assistant steward.

---

*Illiterate. Signed the New Orleans Protest (a sworn declaration of the events of the mutiny) with an "X."

Six female house servants. Two are named: Rachel Glover, aged thirty; and Mary, a mulatto, about thirteen.

Passengers:
Captain Ensor's wife and daughter, aged four.
Captain Ensor's niece, aged fifteen.
William Henry Merritt, acting as a guard over the slaves in exchange for passage to New Orleans.
John R. Hewell, from Richmond, Virginia. Thomas McCargo's agent acting as guard of the thirty-nine slaves owned by McCargo on the *Creole*. The only person killed in the mutiny.
Theophilus McCargo, nephew of Thomas McCargo; he was too young to be an official guard.
Joseph Leitner or Leidner, a Prussian acting as assistant steward in exchange for passage to New Orleans.

In the hold:
One hundred twenty-nine or more men and women slaves being shipped for sale in New Orleans. About one-third of the slaves were women.

The Mutineers on the Creole

Horace Beverley.
Walter Brown.
George Burden.
Richard Butler.
Adam Carnay. Died in the Nassau prison.
Pompey Garrison.
George Grundy. Wounded in the *Creole* affray. Died in the Nassau prison.
William Jenkins.
Ben [the Blacksmith] Johnstone or Johnson. One of Washington's lieutenants.
Philip Jones.
Robert Lumpkins.
Elijah Morris. One of Washington's lieutenants.
George Portlock.
Doctor Ruffin, at times referred to as D. Ruffin. One of Washington's lieutenants.
Peter Smallwood.
Warner Smith.
Addison Tyler.
Madison Washington. Leader of the mutiny.
America or American Wordhouse.

I

"We Have Commenced"

ON THE NIGHT of November 7, 1841, the *Creole*, a brig transporting at least 135 slaves from Richmond, Virginia, to the auction block in New Orleans, was about 130 miles northeast of Hole-in-the-Wall on the northern Bahamian island of Abaco. In the early darkness the captain ordered the brig laid to. There was a fresh breeze, the sky was a little hazy, and trade clouds were flying. The captain and his family, the passengers, some of the crew, and presumably the slaves had all turned in for the night. The ship was dark except for a lantern hanging in the bow.

Zephaniah C. Gifford, first mate of the *Creole*, was on watch at 9 p.m., when Elijah Morris, a slave, came from the forward hold where the male slaves were housed. Morris shouted that one of the slaves had gone into the aft hold which held the forty or so female slaves. Gifford called for help from William Henry Merritt, acting as a guard in exchange for passage to New Orleans. Merritt came from the stateroom where he was sleeping and went to the main hatch, the entrance to the afterhold. There he asked two or three of the slaves if any men were in the hold. He was told there were. Slave men were strictly forbidden from going into the women's quarters, but Gifford and Merritt did not seem to be alarmed. They assumed that one or more slave men were having sex with the women, and that the activities must be interrupted and the men ordered whipped and returned to their own section.

Merritt had an unlighted lamp in his hand, and as soon as Gifford gave him a match he went below and lit it. As the light grew, Merritt found Madison Washington, who was, according to testimony in the New Orleans Protest, "a very large and strong slave belonging to Thomas McCargo, standing at his back."

Merritt said to Washington, "Doctor, you are the last person I would expect to find here." Washington, well known on the *Creole*, was head cook for the slaves and may have been called "Doctor" because he was literate.

Washington responded, "Yes, sir, it is me," and he immediately jumped through the hatchway onto the deck, saying, "I am going up; I cannot stay here." Both Gifford and Merritt laid hands on him, but Merritt had the lighted lamp in one hand, and there was danger of fire should he drop it. The two men could not restrain the powerful Washington, who ran forward. Elijah Morris appeared out of the shadows with a pistol, fired it, and the ball grazed the back of Gifford's head.

Washington then shouted to his slave followers in the forward hold, "We have commenced and must go through; rush, boys, rush aft, we have got them now." Realizing how frightened many of them were, he called out, "Come up, every damned one of you; if you don't and lend a hand, I will kill you all and throw you overboard."

I I

Madison Washington:
Before the Mutiny

A RUNAWAY SLAVE who made his way to Canada in late 1839 or early 1840 as a free man under British protection used the name Madison Washington. But was this his birth name? Was he somehow connected to the slave-owning families of Presidents Washington and Madison? Or had this elegant name been given to him by a plantation owner? Was it more likely that this fugitive slave, for protection, dropped his birth name and assumed one more to his own liking? We do not know. Unfortunately Frederick Douglass, William Wells Brown, and Lydia Maria Child, all contemporaries of Madison Washington and all in a position to write more about his identity and his life before the mutiny, did not do so.

The most accurate biographical information about Madison Washington appears in a brief, unsigned article in the publication *Friend of Man* and is reprinted in *The Liberator* of June 10, 1842. That article indicates that Washington was born in Virginia but gives no locale. Did he work in the fields? in the stables? in the plantation house? Was he a skilled workman—a carpenter, a blacksmith? Did he live in a town instead of in the country? There is no credible evidence to answer these questions in any contemporary accounts. We know that Washington was married, but the *Friend of Man* article does not provide his wife's name. Frederick Douglass, the first important writer to tell Washington's story, though in fictional form, gives her the name of Susan.

Did the Washingtons have children? Again, we do not know. Douglass mentions their two children early on in his story "The Heroic Slave," but he does not refer to them in later chapters. Was Washington mistreated during his years as a slave? The known conditions of slavery and Washington's obviously rebellious nature, independence, and determination to be free make the answer "yes" a given, but we have no direct evidence of his hardship or harsh treatment in slavery. From what we see of him in the official records, he seems to have been young when he first escaped bondage, and it is reasonable to believe that he was born in the second decade of the nineteenth century.

The *Friend of Man* article, quoting members of the Hiram Wilson family in Canada, describes Madison Washington as "like the 'creole protestants' . . . a very large and strong slave," but offers no other details. Did he have a white father as Frederick Douglass and many other slaves did? Or was he "pure" African? Did he have light skin or dark skin? The stereotype illustrations used by Southern newspapers in advertisements for runaway male slaves show a black man without recognizable features, followed by a description giving age, size, prominent features such as a missing front tooth, speech peculiarities or defects, and dress. Because of lack of information, we must see Madison Washington as if he were the newspaper stereotype, but without the printed description.

Why did Madison Washington run away from Virginia? Was his quest for freedom caused in part by mistreatment? Fear of being sold and transported to the slave market in New Orleans? Why could he not take his wife with him? Frederick Douglass and the writers that followed him speculated about the answers

One of the stereotype illustrations manufactured in New York City for the Southern market and used on handbills offering rewards for runaway slaves. Northern businesses had many direct connections with the slave economy. [From *The Anti-Slavery Record*, July 1837, published by the American Anti-Slavery Society]

to these and many other questions concerning Washington's early life, but the explanations are apparently fiction.

The *Friend of Man* article offers no clues to Washington's personality. John Hope Franklin and Loren Schweninger, in *Runaway Slaves*, note that runaways shared many similar traits: "self-confidence, self-assurance, self-possession, determination, and self-reliance. They were resourceful, willful, focused, and purposeful. A number were quick-witted, wily, and intelligent, while most were deceptive and calculating, and not a few were duplicitous and scheming when it came to dealing with whites. Perhaps the most salient characteristic, however, was courage. . . ." From what we see of his activities on the *Creole*, Washington had many of these generalized personality traits, and we know that he had to make use of a great many of them as he made his way successfully from Virginia to Canada.

As a runaway, did Madison Washington travel overland or did he escape by ship? Some captains could be bribed to carry slaves by river and sea to freedom. This was true for Harriet A. Jacobs in 1842. According to her account in *Incidents in the Life of a Slave Girl*, she and her friend Fanny were stowed away in a small ship cabin. Fanny arrived first: "This accommodation had been purchased," Jacobs wrote, "at a price that would pay for a voyage to England. But when one proposes to go to fine old England, they stop to calculate whether they can afford the cost of the pleasure; while in making a bargain to escape from slavery, the trembling victim is making ready to say, 'Take all I have, only don't betray me.'"

Harriet arrived next, the captain having been "handsomely paid." The elderly captain explained why he was aiding the two slaves: he was by birth a Southerner, and his brother was a slave trader. "But," he told them, "it is a pitiable and degrading business, and I always felt ashamed to acknowledge my brother in connection with it." The captain did not betray the two women, but he also profited greatly from his efforts on their behalf.

Other runaways planned escapes in small vessels. According to William Still, the free black man who worked at the Philadelphia Vigilance Committee that aided runaways, in 1860, probably in May, six slaves in Worcester County, Maryland, decided

Left and right, Ellen and William Craft, years after they escaped from Georgia. Center, a portrait of Ellen Craft disguised as a Southern planter. She escaped using William Craft as valet to herself as a "young gentleman."

to acquire a boat and cross the Delaware Bay to New Jersey and freedom. For six dollars they bought a bateau and set out at night. When they were near Kate's Hammock, on the Delaware shore, they were attacked by five white men, also in a boat. The white men attempted to seize the bateau, but the escaping slaves resisted. The inhabitants of both vessels began to fight with oars, and soon the white men retreated and then shot at the fugitives, slightly wounding several of them. The blacks rowed on to New Jersey, where they were assisted and transferred to the Underground Railroad to reach their final destination in Canada.

Some runaways stowed away on oceangoing ships or river boats, but without protection by the captain or a member of the crew they were always in great danger of being discovered. For runaways, the overland route was the more common one.

Some slaves used elaborate ruses to flee the South. William Craft and his wife Ellen, in Macon, Georgia, adopted disguises. She was almost white, and the two decided she would pose as a "gentleman" on a trip north, accompanied by her faithful black slave. They knew they would need to register in hotels and to make many appearances in public during their long trip. They decided that Ellen should be disguised as a young planter who was ill, even infirm. "He must have his right arm placed carefully in a sling," Still wrote in *The Underground Rail Road*, "that would be a sufficient excuse for not registering, etc. Then he must be a little lame, with a nice cane in his left hand; he must have large green spectacles over his eyes, and withal he must be very hard of hearing and dependent on his faithful servant . . . to look after all his wants."

On the steamer from Savannah to Charleston, South Carolina, a slave dealer at dinner said to "Gentleman" Craft about her attentive slave: "I would not take a nigger to the North under no consideration. I have had a deal to do with niggers in my time, but I never saw one who ever had his heel upon free soil that was worth a d—m." The Crafts acted their parts perfectly and after several days of travel arrived in a free state.

The slave John S. Jacobs, Harriet's brother, was taken by his owner on his honeymoon. John's owner had been Harriet's lover and was the father of her two children. The bride was a young woman from Chicago. While in New York, John served dinner to the newlyweds and then walked away. He had previously smuggled his belongings out of the hotel, and he immediately left for New Bedford, Massachusetts. Later, at an anti-slavery meeting, the escaped slave told his story (as reported in *The Liberator,* on August 18, 1848, in the third person) about his escape from his master, a member of the House of Representatives in Washington, D.C.: "His massa, while doting upon a newly married wife, whom he became acquainted with at Washington, and with whom he came North to be joined to, was sufficiently in love to be a little blind in one eye, while the mulatto's suavity in manner pulled the wool over the other."

There were other ruses. The daring Henry Brown of Rich-

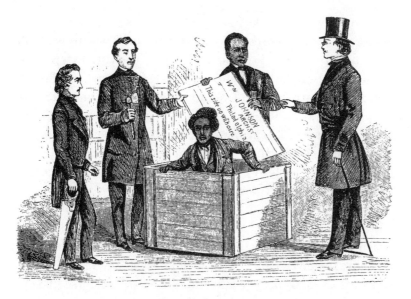

The resurrection of Henry "Box" Brown.

mond, Virginia, ordered a wooden box twenty-four inches wide, thirty-two inches deep, and thirty-six inches long, entered it, and shipped himself to freedom. He had stocked his box with a bladder of water and a few biscuits. After he was nailed into it, the box was shipped to Philadelphia by Adams Express. The usual notices "This Side Up" and "Handle with Care" were sometimes ignored. During the twenty-six-hour trip the box was often handled roughly, and for part of the trip Brown was upside down.

Once the box arrived in Philadelphia, the hickory hoops were cut, the lid taken off, and Brown emerged. According to Still's account in *The Underground Rail Road*, Brown said that "before leaving Richmond he had selected for his arrival-hymn (if he lived) the Psalm beginning with these words: 'I waited patiently for the Lord and He heard my prayer.'"

John Brown in his *Slave Life in Georgia* gives this account of his more traditional escape by land: "My plan was to walk all night, and to hide myself in the day. I used to listen with painful attention for the sounds of footsteps, and when I heard, or fancied I heard a noise, I would conceal myself behind a log, or in a tree, or anywhere else, until the party had gone by, or my fears were allayed. I kept myself from starving by grubbing up sweet potatoes out of the fields by the way-side, which I cooked in a fire I made with dry sticks." Traveling at night was common for most escaped slaves; they followed the North Star for direction.

Madison Washington's escape route is unknown. Possibly he carried forged papers for his protection. If he went overland, he may have received some help from other slaves, from free blacks, or even from a Quaker abolitionist, though Quakers were not numerous in the South. In most cases runaways had no help from whites until they crossed into a free state. Most foraged in fields and gardens and woods as best they could. They feared snakes and wild animals in the forests. They were at the mercy of barking dogs in farmyards and, more ominously, bloodhounds in the early days of their escape as their masters attempted to capture them. Patrols were on the roads, forcing the escapees to seek safety in the woods.

Escaped slaves who were stopped by posses, patrols, or slave catchers often fought desperately, using their fists or sticks, knives, or guns. William Still, in his estimable *The Underground Rail Road*, tells the story of Barnaby Grigsby and his wife Mary Elizabeth, Frank Wanzer, and Emily Foster, all of whom escaped from Loudon County, Virginia, on Christmas Eve, 1855. They took their master's carriage and horses and were joined by two other runaways on horseback. After about a hundred miles, and in brutally cold weather, they were stopped by six white men and a boy who demanded that the slaves surrender. Still describes the scene:

"At this juncture, the fugitives verily believing that the time had arrived for the practical use of their pistols and dirks, pulled them out of their concealment—the young women as well as the young men—and declared they would not be 'taken!' One of the white men raised his gun, pointing the muzzle directly towards one of the young women, with the threat that he would 'shoot,' etc. 'Shoot! shoot! shoot!!!' she exclaimed with a double-barreled pistol in one hand and a long dirk knife in the other, utterly unterrified and fully ready for a death struggle. The male *leader* of the fugitives by this time had 'pulled back the hammers' of his 'pistols' and was about to fire! Their adversaries seeing the weapons, and the unflinching determination on the part of the *runaways* to stand their ground, 'spill blood, kill, or die,' rather than be 'taken,' very prudently 'sidled over to the other side of the road,' leaving at least four of the victors to travel on their way." The two men on horseback, perhaps unarmed, were apparently captured.

The four escapees made their way to Canada, but Frank Wanzer had left relatives behind and decided to rescue them or "die in the attempt." With twenty-two dollars in one pocket and three pistols in other pockets, he made his way back to Virginia and liberated his sister, her husband, and a friend.

Would more slaves have been successful if they had been armed when they made their escapes? Was Madison Washington armed when he made his flight from Virginia? We do not know.

Once Washington reached a free state he was still not out of danger; there were slave catchers everywhere and ready, in anticipation of a reward, to recapture him. He probably tried to find his way to a station on the Underground Railroad. There he would find Quakers or other activists, including blacks, who would provide a safe hiding place, food, and clothes before he could be conducted, usually at night, to the next station and finally his destination in Canada. Resourceful person that he appears to have been, Madison Washington may have made his way to Canada without help from whites or blacks.

He stayed in Canada about a year, according to the *Friend of Man* article, "long enough to love and rejoice in British liberty." Joseph Taper, a slave in Virginia who ran away about the same time Washington did, also made it to Canada with his family. His letter to a white person in Virginia, dated November 11, 1840, expands our knowledge of how slaves felt about their new country: "Since I have been in the Queens dominions I have been well contented, Yes well contented for Sure, man is as God intended he should be. That is, all are born free & equal. This is a wholesome law, not like the Southern laws which puts man made in the image of God, on level with brutes." Taper had a successful year in farming; his five-year-old son was in school and reading. Taper ended his letter with the description of a scene not possible for Washington, whose wife remained in bondage: "My wife and self are sitting by a good comfortable fire happy, knowing that there are none to molest [us] or make [us] afraid."

Although the Taper family appears to have been flourishing in Canada, runaway slaves found themselves in a harsh climate there and were not always well treated by the local white citizens. Levi Coffin, the Quaker abolitionist known as president of the Underground Railroad, visited fugitive slave settlements in Canada in 1844. He wrote: "We found many of the fugitives more comfortably situated than we expected, but there was much destitution and suffering among those who had recently come in." Many of these, he noted, "arrived weary and footsore, with their clothing in rags, having been torn by briers and bit-

William Still worked with the Pennsylvania Vigilance Committee, interviewed hundreds of escaped slaves, and kept extensive notes. He published the narratives of the escapees in *The Underground Rail Road* (1872).

ten by dogs on their way, and when the precious boon of freedom was obtained, they possessed of little else. . . ." Coffin believed there were then about forty thousand fugitive slaves in Canada, but that number is perhaps too high.

Once Madison Washington reached Canada, the *Friend of Man* article notes, "He staid awhile in the family of Hiram Wilson. . . ." This suggests that Washington had help from abolitionists who recommended that he seek out Wilson. During Wilson's student days at Lane Seminary in Cincinnati in 1834, he had been part of a radical group of students and faculty who were warned by the trustees of the institution not to become involved in anti-slavery protests and activities. The so-called "Lane Rebels" thereupon left for the more liberal Oberlin College. Two years later Wilson traveled to Canada to investigate the lives of fugitive slaves there. In 1837, with the help of the

American Anti-Slavery Society and five students at Oberlin, he began to found schools in Canada to educate the former slaves. In 1839 he worked with slaves in Amherstburg, and later he was associated with the Dawn community. Money was always a problem for the Wilson-founded schools. He borrowed heavily—and perhaps unwisely at times—to support his ventures. At one time "he was trusting in the Lord to pay a debt of $10,000."

Wilson's work was practical as well as utopian. As a way of preparing former slaves for their lives in freedom, be believed in manual labor institutes and in education. He wanted the runaways to learn skills that would allow them to have "a full place" in white society. Some fugitives recognized, however, that "distinctions based on skin color . . . would be infinitely slow to pass" and saw the Wilson schools and communities as safe refuges.

Since Wilson was particularly interested in education, he undoubtedly began to teach Washington to read and write. Washington's literacy probably helps explain why members of the crew of the *Creole* called him "Doctor." As Robin Winks noted in *The Blacks in Canada*, "A firm belief in education, and the instant status it gave, lay behind the many assumed titles, the Doctors, Professors and Reverends who sprang so quickly from black soil." But Washington may have had healing abilities, using African or American folk remedies, which would have given him legitimate reasons for assuming the title of doctor.

Wilson's coworker in Canada from 1836 on was Josiah Henson, said by many to have been a model for Harriet Beecher Stowe's character Uncle Tom. Henson had been born a slave in Maryland in 1789, became a Christian at the age of eighteen, and fathered a dozen children. He obeyed his white master, even conducting eighteen slaves from Maryland to Kentucky.

He did not flee to Ohio, a free state, when he was near the end of that trip, nor did he allow his charges to do so. For a long time he acted in what he believed to be the best interests of his master and was loyal and subservient. He thought his master was a fair man, even though when Henson was trying to buy his freedom, his owner cheated him. Still he did not flee. On a trip to New Orleans, however, he had a change of heart. Although he was told he was making the trip to accompany his owner's nephew, he came to realize that the real purpose of the trip was that he himself was to be sold. He was saved from the auction block only because the nephew became seriously ill and asked Henson to bring him back to Kentucky. Henson then resolved to flee to Canada and did so in 1830 with his wife and children.

Most of the eighteen slaves Henson delivered to Kentucky were sold. He saw some of them later on a trip south and realized how wrong he had been in not allowing them to flee. He wrote in his autobiography: "Often since that day has my soul been pierced with bitter anguish, at the thought of having been thus instrumental, in consigning to the infernal bondage of slavery, so many fellow beings. . . . Those were the days of my ignorance. I knew not then the glory of free manhood, or that the title deed of the slave owner is robbery and outrage."

Harriet Beecher Stowe in *Uncle Tom's Cabin* certainly did not portray Henson in the light of his change of heart; she wrote of an Uncle Tom filled with Christian meekness, justifying his refusal to run away. At the beginning of Stowe's novel, Tom's wife urges him to escape rather than be sold. "No, no," he responds, "I ain't going. . . . If I must be sold . . . let me be sold. I s'pose I can b'ar it as well as any on 'em."

There is no evidence that Washington and Henson met, but it seems certain that Washington would have heard about Henson and his experiences in slavery and freedom from Wilson himself.

Most of the escaped slaves in inland Canada around 1840 worked in farming. Tobacco had been a successful crop earlier, but a precipitous drop in prices made it a poor choice when Washington was there. Some work was to be found in logging and in the milling of lumber, but most of the blacks in the various Canadian provinces were general farmers or worked for white farmers in the neighborhood. Joseph Taper wrote in 1840 that his Canadian garden had been a success, with "316 bushels potatoe, 120 bushels corn, 41 bushels buckwheat, a small crop of oats." He also had 17 hogs and 70 chickens. He gave full credit to the British for his freedom and for his new life: "God save Queen Victoria, The Lord bless her in this life, & crown her with glory in the world to come is my prayer." Washington would have known about the successes of farmers such as Taper, but he did not stay in Canada long enough to homestead. It is likely that he did manual work for white farmers or loggers after or during the time he lived with the Wilsons.

We do not know Washington's reactions to Wilson, but we do know from the *Friend of Man* article why he left. After Washington had been in Canada for some time, "long enough to rejoice in British liberty," he realized "he loved his wife, who was left a slave in Virginia, still more."

The historical record does not tell us about Madison Washington's psychological state at this time, but William Still in *The Underground Rail Road* writes about another escaped slave in a situation similar to Washington's. Isaac Forman, twenty-three and a "dark mulatto," was owned by a widow in Norfolk, Virginia, who hired him out. He served as a steward on the steamship *Augusta*. Forman's wife lived in Richmond, and he was denied the privilege of living with her and was allowed to see her only once or twice a year. Fearing that his wife would disapprove, he concealed from her his plans to escape. He was helped by Still in Philadelphia and made his way to Toronto, where he wrote to Still on May 7, 1854: "My soul is vexed, my troubles are inexpressible. I often feel as if I were willing to die. I must see my wife in short, if not, I will die. What would I not give no tongue can utter. Just to gaze on her sweet lips one moment I would be willing to die the next. I am determined to see her some time or other. The thought of being a slave again is miserable. I hope heaven will smile upon me again, before I am one again. I will leave Canada again shortly. . . . If I had known as much before I left, as I do now, I would never have left until I could have found means to have brought her with me. . . . What is freedom to me, when I know that my wife is in slavery?" Still apparently knew nothing else about Forman's plans to see his wife.

It is not difficult to believe that Washington was at times as despondent and depressed as Forman was when he thought of his wife still in bondage. Unlike Forman, Washington does not seem to have contemplated the possibility of returning to Virginia to be reenslaved as a way of being reunited with his wife. Out of love he would act to rescue her, and this desire to free her endeared him to the abolitionists of the 1840s.

Madison Washington left Canada some time in 1841, heading south, seemingly traveling the Underground Railroad in reverse. We see him next in Rochester, New York, where, according to the *Friend of Man* article, "he fell in with friend Lindley Murray Moore." Moore, a Quaker teacher, was later president of the Rochester Anti-Slavery Society. Moore's wife, Abigail, was a member of the abolitionist Mott family. The Moore house seems to have been a station on the railroad Washington was traveling.

Did Washington and the Moores talk about nonviolent approaches to the abolition of slavery favored by the Society of

Friends? We do not know, but later, during the mutiny on the *Creole*, Washington did save many lives. His violence may have been tempered with a humane philosophy.

What we do know is that Moore went around Rochester collecting money for the fugitive and gave him ten dollars. The *Friend of Man* article states Washington's determination clearly: "he assured his friends he would have his wife or lose his life." Frederick Douglass lived in Rochester when he wrote about Washington and the *Creole* revolt, and he knew Moore. Did Douglass get information about Washington's early life from Moore? There is no evidence on this point.

When we hear of Washington next he is in Utica, New York, meeting with Henry Highland Garnet (1815–1882), the minister who had been born in slavery. Garnet's radical stances were far different from the nonviolent wing of abolitionism headed by William Lloyd Garrison and also from the Society of Friends. In 1843, in his rousing speech "An Address to the Slaves of the United States of America," Garnet was urging slaves to arm themselves and end slavery through rebellion. Washington met Garnet two years before that speech, but Garnet in 1841 was already a firebrand who exhorted slaves: "Brethren, arise, arise! Strike for your lives and liberties. Now is the day and hour. Let every slave throughout the land do this and the days of slavery are numbered." Did the two men talk of violent methods for ending slavery?

Garnet, even as a young man, stood up for his rights and was not afraid to use a gun. In 1835 he enrolled in the Noyes Academy in Canaan, New Hampshire, a school for African-American males. Local farmers, enraged that a "nigger school" was in their midst, attacked it. The black students were saved when Garnet fired a double-barreled shotgun at the attackers. The school was destroyed, but Garnet's active response kept the ruffians and bullies from killing or injuring the students. If

Robert Purvis

Garnet did not tell Washington about his experiences at Noyes Academy, it is likely that others along the Underground Railroad would have recounted this story as justifying the successful use of violence.

In a speech delivered in Cork, Ireland, on October 23, 1845, Frederick Douglass said that Garnet advised Washington against going back to Virginia because it would be pointless. Douglass had met Garnet and probably knew of the Garnet-Washington conversation directly from Garnet. Washington must have told Garnet the story of his life in Virginia, his escape, his life in Canada, and his love for his wife. But Douglass includes no detailed information about this crucial conversation which likely took place between the two men in Utica.

Somewhere on his trip south or in Canada, Washington also met John Gurney (1788–1847), the wealthy English Quaker emancipationist who traveled in the United States and Canada from 1837 to 1840. Douglass, in his "Slavery, the Slumbering Volcano" speech, delivered in New York on April 23, 1849, reported that Gurney also advised Washington not to go to Virginia to try to rescue his wife.

In that same speech Douglass reported that Robert Purvis (1810–1898), the wealthy black who lived on an estate in Byberry near Philadelphia, also met Washington on his trip back to Virginia. Purvis's English father was a successful cotton broker in Charleston, and his mother was of German and Moroccan ancestry. Purvis had been educated at Amherst and became a leading abolitionist, closely allied with Garrison.

Douglass certainly knew Purvis, and in the "Slumbering Volcano" speech his comments about the meeting between Washington and Purvis must have come directly from Purvis. According to Douglass, Purvis advised Washington "not to go, and for a time he was inclined to listen to his counsel. He told him it would be of no use for him to go, for that as sure as he went he would only be himself enslaved, and could of course do nothing towards freeing his wife. Under the influence of his counsel he consented not to go; but when he left the house of Purvis, the thoughts of his wife in Slavery came back to his mind to trouble his peace and disturb his slumbers. So he resolved again to take no counsel either on the one hand or the other, but to go back to Virginia and rescue his wife if possible."

Because Douglass knew Moore, Garnet, Gurney, and Purvis, and given his interest in Washington's story, he must have over the years asked for details about the conversations these abolitionists may have had with Washington. It would appear, though, that Douglass kept much of that information to himself. His insistence in his speeches that Garnet, Gurney, and Purvis advised Washington not to return to Virginia to rescue his wife, may have served Douglass's rhetorical purposes.

What prospects did Washington face in his quest to be reunited with his wife? Had he been a trained artisan, he might have made enough money to purchase her, but the record does

A Quaker, Levi Coffin, was often called the president of the Underground Railroad. His *Reminiscences* (1876) are a valuable historical record of his work with fugitive slaves.

not indicate he had such skills. He could have attempted to raise money from abolitionists or their sympathizers, but that too would have been difficult, because most of the abolitionists he met (Gurney and Purvis excepted) were not wealthy. The conductors on the Underground Railroad—and he must have met many of them as he journeyed southward—gave as much as they could from their own funds to many destitute runaways. For Madison Washington to have raised the eight hundred dollars or more needed to purchase his wife would have been almost impossible. Levi Coffin reported that he "was often called upon to aid persons who had obtained their liberty, to buy their wife or husband or children out of slavery." When there was "little probability of success," Coffin "discouraged the effort," but he did help when it was likely that funds could be raised.

Washington, had he been lucky, might have found someone to help him regain his wife. Henson returned to Kentucky to lead slaves to freedom, but Henson knew Kentucky, giving him a distinct advantage, and we have no proof that Washington met Henson. The case of John White is particularly instructive as we consider Madison Washington's options. White, a slave, lived in Kentucky, across the Ohio River from Rising Sun, Indiana. He was married to a slave who was the daughter of her master. John belonged to another master, but he often visited his wife and children. When he learned he was to be sent south for sale, he ran away to Indiana and was helped for several weeks by Levi Coffin, who found him "bright and intelligent, but his mind seemed overclouded with gloom at the prospect of leaving his family in slavery."

White was sent on to Canada, for it was usually unsafe for fugitives to stay close to the slave state from which they had escaped. Slave catchers were always to be found in those nearby free areas, working vigorously to capture and return runaways. White stopped first in Adrian, Michigan, at the Raisin Institute, a school open to all and directed by Laura S. Haviland, a Quaker friend of Coffin's. He then went on to Canada but stayed only a short time there before returning to the Raisin Institute where he studied and waited for the appropriate time to try to rescue his wife and children.

When summer came, White returned to Newport, Indiana, where Coffin lived. His first efforts to free his family failed, and he worked and attended school for a time before returning to the Raisin Institute to continue his education. Laura Haviland, who had become interested in helping rescue White's family, went to Rising Sun herself to see what might be done. She disguised herself as an aunt of John's wife, who was almost white, and with berry pails over each arm received permission from the master to pick blackberries with her niece. In the berry patch, she told John's wife about her husband's hopes to rescue her and the children. Arrangements were hurriedly made for the escape. A skiff was brought to the Kentucky side of the Ohio River, and a wagon was to be waiting for the woman and her children on the Indiana side. John's wife gathered her children and fled to the skiff where John was waiting for them. The currents were swift, and when they could not reach the Indiana side, they were forced back to the Kentucky banks of the river. Meanwhile the wife's master/father had organized a posse, and the woman and her children were recaptured. John escaped briefly but was soon captured and jailed. He gave a false name and was not recognized. Coffin and Haviland were able to get him released from jail for $350.

According to Levi Coffin, John White returned to Michigan a heartbroken man. He was never to see his wife and children again, for they were sold and separated. Haviland wrote to John's wife's master/father several times about his "sin of selling his own child" and, of course, his grandchildren. Her letters impressed him, Coffin wrote, and he almost went insane: "he would walk the floor of nights, hour after hour, striving to make terms with his guilty conscience." He tried to repurchase his daughter and grandchildren but failed. Just how many slave owners were conscience-stricken after the sale of their own children is not known, but it was probably not a large number.

Levi Coffin apparently did not know John's emotional state after the runaway's final defeat in rescuing his wife and children, but we can assume he was "overclouded with gloom." Madison Washington was also to fail in his attempt to rescue his wife, and his emotional state may well have played a part in the mutiny he organized on the *Creole*.

In the South there were a few professional slave stealers,

abolitionists who secretly took slaves from slave owners and helped them escape to freedom, but Washington apparently knew none of them. Levi Coffin recounted the career of John Fairfield, a Virginian who was opposed to slavery though he came from a slave-owning family. As a young man he decided to bring his slave friend Bill away from bondage. They were the same age and had played together as children. Fairfield took two horses from his uncle, and he and his friend reached Canada. He told Coffin that he felt no guilt about stealing the horses, for Bill had earned several. "As to negro-stealing," Fairfield said, "I would steal all the slaves in Virginia if I could."

Returning to Virginia, Fairfield stole more slaves before returning to Canada, where former slaves, hearing of his exploits, began to ask him to steal their wives, children, or other relatives. Coffin is not clear about the dates that Fairfield was liberating slaves, but it seems to have begun after Washington was in Canada. Fairfield would have been the ideal person to bring Washington's wife away from Virginia, for he knew the terrain and the people of that state.

Fugitive slaves who asked for Fairfield's help would give him money if they had it, but if necessary he would work without pay for the thrill of the escapade. He was, as Coffin observed, "fond of adventure and excitement." He was always heavily armed and never hesitated to use his weapons. Coffin believed that in twelve years Fairfield had helped thousands of slaves escape. Coffin said of him, "He was a wicked man, daring and reckless in his actions," but Coffin knew that he was always faithful to slaves and sincerely hated the institution of slavery. Although Coffin had no sympathy for Fairfield's methods, he always aided the slaves Fairfield had liberated. Coffin told him to love his enemies and refuse to kill. Fairfield responded: "Love the devil! Slaveholders are all devils, and it is no harm to kill the devil. I do not intend to hurt people if they keep out of the way, but if they step in between me and liberty, they must take the consequences. When I undertake to conduct slaves out of bondage I feel that it is my duty to defend them, even to the last drop of blood."

Some well-known slave snatchers, however, would have been reluctant to help Washington liberate his wife. John P. Parker (1827–1900), for example, was born to a white man and a slave woman in Virginia. At the age of eight he was marched in a group to Mobile, Alabama. He became a skilled iron worker and made enough money to buy his freedom and move to Indiana. He then began to rescue slaves. The *Cincinnati Commercial Tribune* said of Parker: "a more fearless creature never lived. He gloried in danger. . . . He would go boldly over into the enemy's camp and filch the fugitives to freedom." A slave who had escaped to Canada was on his way back to a slave state to get his wife when he came to Parker for help. "I tried to persuade him to get another wife," Parker said.

Parker was speaking more harshly than those who were urging Madison Washington not to venture into Virginia to rescue his wife. Garnet, Gurney, and Purvis might have offered to help Washington get a good-paying job that would allow him to save money to buy his wife. They might have put him in touch with a slave stealer who would help him. They could have set up a committee to raise funds to buy Washington's wife. Apparently they did none of these things. They could not understand Washington's powerful love for his wife.

Moore, Garnet, Gurney, and Purvis had different approaches to the abolition of slavery. Moore and Gurney were Quakers and held firm views against violent acts. Purvis, a Garrisonian, also believed in nonviolent measures, but it should be noted that Garrison's language was filled with violence. Garnet was a firm believer in the necessity of force to abolish slavery. At various times during the mutiny on the *Cre-*

ole, Washington used elements of all these various approaches: he could be both violent and humane, as the situation dictated.

In his quest to free his wife, Washington might have used a duplicitous approach. Levi Coffin told the story of the cunning slave Jim, from Kentucky. When Jim decided to seek his freedom, he did not tell his wife or his fellow slaves about his intentions. He made it across the river to the Ohio shore and was put on the underground route to Canada, but he did not remain long in Canada before he felt an urge to return to the South. He told Coffin: "Oh, how sweet it was to breathe free air, to feel that I had no massa who could whip me or sell me. But I was not happy long. I could not enjoy liberty when the thoughts of my poor wife and children would rise up before me. I thought to myself, I have learned the way and found friends all along the road; now I will go back and fetch my wife and children. I'll go to old massa's plantation, and I'll make believe I am tired of freedom. . . . I will go to work hard and watch for a chance to slip away my wife and children."

That is exactly what Jim did. As Coffin told the story, Jim presented himself at the plantation and to his master: he "made a low bow, and stood before him as humble as a whipped dog." He told a story the master wanted to and could believe: "I found that Canada was no place for niggers; it's too cold, and we can't make any money there. Mean white folks cheat poor niggers out of their wages when they hire them. . . . And those people called abolitionists, that I met with on the way, are a mean set of rascals. They pretend to help the niggers, but they cheat them all they can."

The master believed these stories, and Jim worked hard to please him. Jim appeared to be telling his fellow slaves about the horrors he had experienced during his months of freedom, though in fact he gave them subtle signals that he was dissembling. In the spring he was able to get his wife and children and some of his slave friends across the Ohio River into Indiana. They were protected by the Coffin family and sent on to Canada. Coffin later visited Jim and his family in Canada, where they lived in a comfortable home. Jim told Coffin that he hoped God would forgive him for telling his master so many lies. He had no feelings of homesickness and certainly "no long- ings for massa and the old plantation in Kentucky."

Madison Washington did not assume the role of trickster in Virginia, nor does it appear that he attempted to locate a slave stealer. He planned to act alone, to become himself a thief in the night, stealing his wife away, a course of action consistent with what is known about his independent and courageous character.

But a slave society in Virginia was ranged against him, and his independence and courage were not enough to prevent his recapture. Most of the details of what happened to Washington once he was back in Virginia are unknown. What we do know is that he was seized and sold to the slave trader Thomas Mc- Cargo.

III

Madison Washington's Capture and Sale

OF MADISON WASHINGTON'S CAPTURE in Virginia, the author of the *Friend of Man* article provides no details. But he infers what happened: "And as it is the custom with slaveholders in the more northern slave States to send the fugitive when received by them to the extreme South—lest he escape again—lest he communicate to other slaves the incidents of his day of freedom—as an example that shall strike terror to the breast of his fellows—he is sold to the southern market." That may indeed be what happened to Washington, but it is only speculation, as no historical evidence has survived. There are no valid accounts of his recapture, punishment, and sale to a slave trader. His psychological state after being captured is nowhere discussed in any of the records. The fate of his wife is unknown.

We can assume that Washington was punished psychologically as well as physically. He was probably forbidden to see his wife and other members of his family. He was perhaps fitted with a spiked collar, chained, and confined in a cramped space, but if his owner wished to get the best price for Washington, he

Scars from a whipping or whippings. [*Harper's Weekly*]

would not want whipping scars to mark him. Such scars told the buyer that the slave was rebellious.

John Brown in *Slave Life in Georgia* explains how whippings were carried out without leaving marks that would "depreciate the value of the 'property.'" Male or female slaves were stripped naked and flogged with a "flopping paddle" made of leather about eighteen inches long and four inches wide. Its wooden handle was about two feet long. The whipper, Brown wrote, "lays on, flop, flop, flop" for thirty minutes of this severe punishment in which no blood is actually drawn. If Washington's master or overseer were particularly cruel and angry at the runaway, he might have branded him or whipped him severely enough to leave permanent scars. Official documents offer no information about Washington's treatment after he was recaptured.

Whether Washington was punished or not in the days after his capture, he would likely have been confined in a local jail or private slave pen until he could be sold. Washington was large and strong, and no plantation, farm, or town dwelling would have had the facilities to secure him.

Once offered for sale, Washington would have been seen by slave traders. As Walter Johnson notes in *Soul by Soul*, the traders would make judgments based on age, sex, skin color, signs of illness, or disfigurements from accidents or punishments. Inspections were a continuation of the kinds of examinations made in Africa before slaves were shipped to the Americas. Theophilus Conneau in a *A Slaver's Log Book* describes this procedure in the African barracoons: men, women, and children were brought in naked, and "all underwent a long manipulation. This was done to ascertain the soundness of their limbs. Every joint was made to crack; hips, armpits, and groins were also examined."

In the South one trader gave this Victorian version of the examinations: "My inspection was made in the usual manner: their coats being taken off and the breast, arms, teeth, and general form and appearance looked at." In viewing rooms, hidden from the auction block, buyers would "run their hands over the slaves, fingering their joints, and kneading their flesh." Both men and women were subject to such treatment.

John Brown in *Slave Life in Georgia* made it clear just how revolting and sexually degrading these examinations were: "I dare not—for decency's sake—detail the various expedients

John Brown, author of *Slave Life in Georgia* (1855).

that are resorted to by dealers to test the soundness of a male or a female slave. When I say that they are handled in the grossest manner, and inspected with the most elaborate and disgusting minuteness, I have said enough for the most obtuse understanding to fill up the outline of the horrible picture. What passes behind the screen of the auction-room, or in the room where the dealer is left alone with the 'chattels' offered to him to buy, only those who have gone through the ordeal can tell."

Cinqué, the African slave who led the mutiny on the ship *Amistad*, testified at the trial in New Haven that when he was in the Havana barracoon José Ruiz, who had bought him, felt him to determine if he was healthy. Cinqué created a stir in the courtroom as he demonstrated just how he had been inspected.

Brown was not reticent about sexual matters when he wrote that in the Goodin and Co. slave pen in New Orleans, where he had been confined, "the youngest and handsomest females were set apart as the concubines of the masters, who generally changed mistresses every week." Use of female slaves as sexual objects would certainly have been the practice in slave pens, slave caravans, and slave transport ships throughout the South during slavery days.

Walter Johnson has perceptively noted, "As they went about their slave-market business, slaveholders mapped their own forbidden desires into slaves' bodies. . . ." A slave woman "indecently '*examined*' in the presence of a dozen or fifteen brutal men" was subjected to "brutal remarks and licentious looks." Clearly the "stated concern about the woman's capacity for reproduction served as public cover for a much more general interest in her naked body." Men's bodies, too, were subjected to erotic inspections, as John Brown insisted. Examinations of the male genitalia in an attempt to detect venereal diseases would have called forth ribald comments about the size of the black penis, supposedly admired and feared by many white Southern males.

In the fall of 1841 slave traders bought slaves in Virginia, then transported this "property" southward to the market in New Orleans. The large Louisiana auctions would proceed during the winter, providing slaves for the coming planting season in the spring. Virginia had more slaves than needed in that area, but slaves were in great demand for the cotton and sugar kingdoms "down South." All through the South, the day of the slave sale was chaotic. Husbands, wives, and children were brutally separated, creating what Brown described as "the most fearful scenes of anguish and confusion . . . converting the auction-room into a perfect Bedlam of despair."

A slave auction at Richmond. [Library of Congress]

...*A* well-known Richmond, Virginia, trader named Thomas McCargo purchased Madison Washington. McCargo's slave "business" consisted of sending the local oversupply of slaves to those areas where they were needed. He appears to have been successful and prosperous and therefore must have traded on a rather large scale, for profits on an individual sale were not large. McCargo's fellow slave trader James H. Birch illegally bought the free man Solomon Northup for $650 and had him sold for $900. Walter Johnson in *Soul by Soul* published sections of John White's account book detailing White's trading activities. He would sometimes buy at $600 and sell for $750, but the $150 difference would have to pay for food, clothing, transportation by ship or land, insurance costs, and slave-pen charges in New Orleans. There were other risks: slaves sometimes died before they could be sold, and while the trader might think he could sell at a profit, the slave might become ill, forcing a sale at a loss. McCargo shipped thirty-nine slaves on the *Creole*. He insured many of them for $800 each, with a premium of 2 percent, or $16. Those slaves he valued at $800 (he may have paid less for them) he undoubtedly expected to sell for $1,000 or more. He may have been preparing another shipment of slaves that fall, for he did not accompany the slaves on the *Creole*.

As Walter Johnson has shown, a few traders who were particularly successful financially were not stigmatized because of the nature of their occupation. Many, perhaps most, traders were known to be sharp, even shady businessmen, and individual owners who dealt with them had reason to distrust them, even though they were necessary to the slave economy.

Daniel Hundley in his *Social Relations in Our Southern States*, a pro-slavery account, wrote, "The miserly Negro Trader is outwardly a coarse, ill-bred person, provincial in speech and manners, with a cross-looking phiz, a whiskey tinctured nose, and cold hard-looking eyes, a dirty tobacco-stained mouth and shabby dress." Readers of *Uncle Tom's Cabin* met such a trader in Haley: "He was a short thick-set man, with coarse commonplace features, and that swaggering air of pretension which marks a low man who is trying to elbow his way upward in the world." Although these descriptions may have been based on stereotypes, they do contain elements of truth.

Hundley described traders in the same way many slaves in their narratives did: the trader, Hundley wrote, "is not troubled evidently with conscience. . . . He habitually separates parent from child, brother from sister, and husband from wife. . . ." Hundley castigated the business practices of the trader: "nearly nine tenths of the slaves he buys and sells are vicious ones sold for crimes or misdemeanors, or otherwise diseased ones sold because of their worthlessness as property.

These he purchases for about one half what healthy and honest slaves would cost him; but he sells them as both honest and healthy."

Although there is truth in Hundley's comments, the Virginia situation in 1840 was somewhat different. Since the state had an oversupply of slaves, many of those being sold were not criminals or runaways or seriously ill. That said, Hundley is correct in noting that the traders were unconscionable in their business of buying and selling blacks. Slave owners themselves were often far from honest in their descriptions of the health and value of their for-sale slaves. Slavery corrupted every institution and person it touched.

McCargo seems to have been a successful trader, but did he have the red nose of the whiskey drinker? Was he coarse and ill-bred? Did he mistreat slaves? Was he unethical in his business dealings? Did he have hard eyes and a tobacco-stained mouth? The record is mostly silent, but we do have—by way of Solomon Northup's *Twelve Years a Slave* and John Brown's *Slave Life in Georgia*—fragments of information about him and chilling details about his fellow slave traders and partners. From them we can surmise that McCargo's treatment of slaves, his business practices, and his demeanor were similar to the others described by Hundley and Stowe.

After Madison Washington's capture, it is certainly possible that he was jailed in Richmond, Virginia, in a slave pen owned by a slave trader named Goodin. Goodin was perhaps part owner of a New Orleans pen named Goodin & Co., managed by another part-owner, Theophilus Freeman. Washington was being sent to Freeman by McCargo, another of Freeman's and Goodin's partners. The slave Solomon Northup, consigned by Goodin to Freeman, made the voyage from Richmond to New Orleans in the spring of 1841, only months before the *Creole* mutiny. From Northup's narrative we have many details about the slave trade in the upper South, about domestic slave ships in 1841, and about slave traders and their slave captives.

Northup (1808–1863?), a mulatto and a free man, lived in Saratoga Springs, New York. He was married and had three children when in late March or early April 1841 he was drugged and kidnapped by two rogues. He awoke to find himself in William H. Williams's slave pen in Washington, D.C. One of the largest slave traders in that city, Williams was a business associate of Freeman's, regularly sending slaves to the Goodin & Co. slave pen in New Orleans for sale there. Northup had been acquired illegally, and knowingly so, by James H. Birch. (In his narrative Northup consistently uses the spelling Burch.) Birch, a Washington slave dealer and a partner of Freeman's, was a notorious trader, unethical and known to be a liar. Northup wrote that Birch's features were "grossly coarse, expressive of nothing but cruelty and cunning."

Northup was placed in a damp cell furnished with a wooden bench and a "dirty box stove." He had no bed, no blanket. The door of the cell led to a yard enclosed by a high brick wall, about thirty feet from the house. As Northup described the pen: "The top of the wall supported one end of a roof, which ascended inwards, forming a kind of open shed. Underneath the roof there was a crazy loft all round, where slaves, if so disposed, might sleep at night, or in inclement weather seek shelter from the storm. It was like a farmer's barnyard in most respects, save it was so constructed that the outside world could never see the human cattle that were herded there."

Northup insisted to Birch that he was a free man. This enraged Birch, who "flew into a towering passion." "With blasphemous oaths" he called Northup "a black liar, a runaway from Georgia, and every other profane and vulgar epithet that the most indecent fancy could conceive." Birch then called for his assistant Ebenezer Radburn, and the two seized Northup,

Solomon Northup, after he was sold in Louisiana.

roughly removed his clothing, and pulled his naked body over the bench in the cell. Birch began the beating, Northup remembered: "Blow after blow was inflicted upon my naked body. When his unrelenting arm grew tired, he stopped and asked if I still insisted I was a free man. I did insist upon it, and then the blows were renewed, faster and more energetically, if possible, than before." Northup felt as if he were on fire: "My sufferings I can compare to nothing else than the burning agonies of hell!" Birch admitted in an 1853 deposition to giving Northup one hundred lashes.

This building in Alexandria, Virginia, housed a slave pen. The sign read "Price, Birch & Co., Dealers in Slaves." Birch probably moved his pen to Alexandria after the Compromise of 1850 halted the slave trade in Washington, D.C. [Library of Congress]

Two weeks after this whipping, early in the morning, Birch came to Williams's pen for the slaves belonging to him and marched them to a steamboat on the Potomac. Northup was already thinking of escape, but he was handcuffed and could not flee. Once the slaves reached the steamboat, they were placed in the hold, and the boat pulled away from the dock. "The bell tolled as we passed the tomb of Washington," Northup wrote with bitter humor. "Burch, no doubt, with uncovered head, bowed reverently before the sacred ashes of the man who devoted his illustrious life to the liberty of his country."

At Aquia Creek, Birch and his five slaves were transferred to

Inside a slave pen. [Library of Congress]

a stage coach destined for Fredericksburg, Virginia. On arrival there they were put on a car for Richmond. Once in Richmond, the slaves were taken to Goodin's yard. Goodin was there—"a short, fat man, with a round, plump face, black hair and whiskers, and a complexion almost as dark as one of his own negroes. He had a hard, stern look. . . ." Goodin and Birch greeted each other cordially, and it is safe to assume that McCargo was also a friend, since all three were partners or business associates of Freeman in New Orleans. Possibly Madison Washington was housed in Goodin's pen a few months after Northup was held there.

49

The pen or yard, Northup wrote, was quite similar to the one owned by Williams in Washington but larger, and there were two small houses at opposite corners where slaves could be examined by prospective purchasers. The pen held about thirty people.

On a rough table under the shed, the slaves had their supper of pork and bread, standard fare for slaves in transit. In New Orleans the food would be better because the traders there wanted the slaves to appear healthy. The slaves stayed in Goodin's yard overnight, and the next day they were marched to the brig *Orleans*, a ship undoubtedly similar to the *Creole*.

The slaves in Birch's gang had been consigned to Theophilus Freeman, managing partner of the Goodin & Co. slave pen in New Orleans. Freeman is described by Northup as a tall, thin-faced man with fair complexion, and "a little bent." He was bent in more ways than in stature. He was, Northup learned immediately, blasphemous and cruel. The slaves were taken to his slave pen, similar to the one in Richmond but much larger still. The yard covered an acre and in "high season" in winter could hold five hundred slaves. John Brown, who had also been held there, reported that a "block of houses" formed a square around the yard. The windows opening to the street were heavily barred. "The houses themselves," Brown remembered, "were built upon brick pillars or piers, the spaces between which had been converted into stores. Of these there were a great number," one of them being used as the living quarters for the traders. McCargo lived on the premises when he was in New Orleans. Slaves were housed in three floors of rooms around the yard.

With the arrival of Northup and the Birch group, only about fifty slaves were being held in Freeman's pen, this being the "off season." By winter the pen would be filled with five hundred or more people, with constant arrivals and departures of slaves and traders.

Northup quickly learned about the "pious hearted" Freeman. The morning after the Birch group arrived, Freeman "was out among his animals early in the morning, with an occasional kick of the older men and women, and many a sharp crack of the whip about the ears of the younger slaves, it was not long before they were all astir, and wide awake." He expected to get them all cleaned up, outfitted with new clothes, and ready for sale that very day. He thought of the slaves not as humans but as farm animals to be groomed before going on the auction block.

Freeman was known for his unethical business practices. He certainly falsified the ages of slaves; when he sold Solomon Northup, he reduced his age by a decade. Perhaps because Northup was a kidnapped free man, he was given another name, Platt, in the official sale record. According to the *Dictionary of Louisiana Biography,* Freeman "also separated young children from their mothers, contrary to Louisiana law, and whipped or kicked slaves in his yard." It was said that he lived as though married to the mulatto laundress Sarah Conner, an ex-slave who had purchased her freedom from Freeman in July 1841. Freeman would receive visitors while lying in bed with his mistress, and he took her along on trips to New York and Philadelphia.

John Brown wrote about how Freeman preyed on slaves. The slave trader met in New Orleans a beautiful mulatto who was both wife and slave of a Natchez man. Freeman had power over her since she was unaccompanied. He forced her to have her trunks sent to his place and to let the public believe she was his property. She stayed two weeks with him. Brown implies that she was Freeman's concubine for that time. Freeman had a changing supply of concubines in his slave pen, but Sarah Conner was his resident mistress.

Freeman was declared insolvent in January 1844, with assets of $137,991 and debts of $186,698. His creditors claimed that he used his mistress Sarah to sequester his two plantations in Louisiana and one in Georgia, that he hid some of his slaves in New Orleans and on his Louisiana plantations, and that he unlawfully withdrew $10,000 from Goodin & Co. and gave that money to someone else for safekeeping. That sum was probably swindled from his partners and business associates. He was arrested several times in 1845, for it was feared he would flee the state. The litigation over his finances went on until 1861 when, in the confusion caused by the Civil War, he left New Orleans and disappeared. That McCargo would have Freeman as a business partner suggests that he tolerated such behavior, at least until he was swindled. McCargo was undoubtedly as cruel to slaves as Birch, Goodin, and Freeman were.

When John Brown was confined to Freeman's slave pen in the mid-1840s, he observed that the youngest and most attractive of the slave women became the concubines of the masters. "The slave-pen," wrote Brown, "is only another name for a brothel." The same could be said of international and domestic slave ships, for the slave women and girls could not protect themselves from white sexual predators. McCargo probably had his temporary mistresses in the Goodin & Co. slave pen, for he sometimes accompanied his slaves to New Orleans.

Sometimes, Northup wrote, Freeman had special merchandise for sale: he said of the seven- or eight-year-old Emily, whom he refused to sell to the man who had purchased Eliza, Emily's mother, "There were heaps and piles of money to be made of her . . . when she was a few years older." Men in New Orleans would pay $5,000 "for such an extra, handsome, fancy

Emily, Eliza, Theophilus Freeman, and William Ford. Solomon
Northup wrote this account of events after Eliza was sold to William
Ford: "She broke from her place in the line of women and rushing
down where Emily was standing, caught her in her arms. . . . Oh! how
piteously then did she beseech and beg and pray that they might not
be separated. Why could they not be purchased together? . . . 'Mercy,
mercy, master!' she cried. . . . 'Please, master, buy Emily. I can never
work any if she is taken from me; I will die.'" Ford agreed to buy
Emily, but Freeman refused to sell the beautiful child. He planned to
sell her in a few years as a concubine.

piece as Emily would be. . . . She was a beauty—a picture—a doll—one of the regular blood—none of your thick-lipped, bullet-headed, cotton picking niggers—if she was might he be d—d." Freeman was counting on the sexual proclivities of some wealthy Southern men to ensure a grand payment for Emily, but it is likely that she would be Freeman's own concubine before he sold her as a guaranteed young virgin.

Although McCargo was seemingly successful economically, he was a gambler and not always aware of his surroundings, perhaps because he was befuddled by drink. Freeman's New Orleans pen, where McCargo housed slaves awaiting sale, contained a gambling saloon. According to John Brown in *Slave Life in Georgia*, he saw McCargo and Freeman in that saloon. McCargo was losing at the gambling table and would go across to his own room to "take a handful of gold out of his trunk, with which he would return, to stake and play again." Brown, himself a slave in the pen, was talking to the rogue who had sold him to Freeman. The two saw where the money was kept and decided to rob McCargo. Brown acted as watch, and the young white man went into McCargo's room, put his hand in the trunk, and took out a handful of gold coins, six of which he gave to Brown. The young man then went into the saloon himself. Brown gives no indication that McCargo ever missed his gold, suggesting he had much to drink that night. Brown admitted to his readers that he may not have been morally justified in participating in the theft, but he felt at the time that there was nothing wrong in his actions because McCargo had acquired the gold by selling "niggers."

The disreputable Thomas McCargo shipped thirty-nine slaves on the *Creole* in October 1841. He may have brought many of them himself to Richmond, perhaps in a caravan called a coffle. One slave gave this graphic description of a cof-

A coffle in the South. [Library of Congress]

fle, which was led by chained resisters and troublemakers: "A long row of men chained two-and-two together . . . numbering about thirty persons, was the first to march forth . . . then came the quiet slaves—that is, those who were tame in spirit and degraded; then came the unmarried women, or those without children; after these came the children who were able to walk; and following them came mothers with their infants and young children in their arms."

The traders and guards of the coffles were outnumbered, and slaves being sent South were not always docile. The slaves in greatest danger of revolting or running away—and that included Madison Washington—were certainly chained. To further prevent revolt, many slave traders forbade the slaves in the coffle to speak among themselves. Some coffles were on the road for days, and to prevent an insurrection, as Johnson has shown in *Soul by Soul*, the guards forced the slaves to sleep in their chains.

Women slaves in the coffle were vulnerable to sexual abuse, as John Brown knew from experience. When he was nearly ten he was sold by the pound to a trader named Sterling Finney and marched away in a coffle. One of Brown's fellow slaves was a young woman of about twenty. Finney forced her into his wagon and "brutally ill-used her and permitted his companions to treat her in the same manner."

Brown reported that the other slave women in the coffle were distressed about the multiple rapes. The memory of this event stayed with the young boy.

Just how prudent Thomas McCargo and his agent John R. Hewell were in guarding the valuable slaves before they were placed on the *Creole* is not known. McCargo certainly did not guard his gold coins well. Did Madison Washington arrive in Richmond in a coffle? We do not know. Down the river, after the *Creole* left Richmond, more McCargo slaves were boarded. Those slaves probably came overland to the dock. Once the McCargo slaves were on the ship they were to be guarded by Hewell, who was apparently fully as cruel as Birch was.

Madison Washington was now caught up in the system of buying and selling slaves, at the mercy of guards in coffles, jails, and slave ships. He was a captive in an inhumane system given over to psychological and physical cruelty. The slave trader who purchased him would send him by domestic slave ship to New Orleans. On that ship he and his fellow slaves would be subjected to some of the same mistreatment his ancestors had suffered on the international slave ships that brought them from Africa to the Americas. These ships and those used for the domestic slave trade had much in common.

I V

The Slave Ships

THE INTERNATIONAL SLAVE TRADE between Africa and the New World developed over centuries and set the pattern for domestic slave transportation by water in the United States and in other slave countries in the Americas. The characteristics of these ships and the slaves they carried help us understand what happened on the *Creole*.

While slavery had long been institutionalized in Africa and in many other parts of the world, the European-African slave trafficking began in the 1440s. From the earliest days, the horrors of that institution were apparent. When 235 slaves were landed in Portugal in 1444, Gomes Eannes de Zumara, a courtier in the service of Prince Henry, wrote: "What heart could be so hard as not to be pierced with piteous feelings to see that company?" The slaves were in great distress, some "crying out loudly, as if asking help from the Father of nature; . . . while others made lamentations in the manner of a dirge. . . ." Their sufferings were increased by "the division of the captives. . . . No respect was shown to either friends or relations, but each fell where his lot took him." That kind of anguish among the slaves remained constant through the next four centuries of the trade.

Because the slave trade brought great profits, many Euro-

Captives in a coffle in Africa. [Harvard College Library]

pean countries became involved in the purchase and sale of Africans. Profit quickly triumphed over conscience and humane feeling. Slaves began to pour into the New World, and few questioned the absolute right of one person to own another person.

After Africans were captured, often by agents of their own or neighboring chieftains, they were marched in coffles to the sea where they were confined in squalid barracoons until they were sold to Europeans or Americans. They were then placed on board slave ships controlled by a captain who had total power over them for the next few weeks. John Newton, the eighteenth-century captain out of Liverpool, later to become an Anglican minister, wrote: "I am as absolute in my small dominions as any potentate in Europe. If I say to one, come, he comes; if to another, go, he flies." The captain's complete control over his ship and its cargo allowed for unspeakable acts of enormous cruelty.

A few captains, including Newton, had qualms about trading in human flesh. Newton wrote, "I know of no method of getting money, not even that of robbing for it upon the highway, which has so direct a tendency . . . to rob the heart of every gentle disposition, and to harden it, like steel." The slave industry was so immensely profitable, however, that most captains refused to acknowledge the harm being done to Africans or to themselves. Consciences were stifled, and captains ruled with the lash and threats and bribes, all of which effectively controlled both the crew and the slaves. Yet they were able to deliver only a percentage of the slaves on board their ships, for many died in the terrible conditions of the slave hold and some took their own lives by jumping into the ocean. Still others attempted to starve themselves to death, though force-feeding kept some of these alive to reach their destination.

The captain and the first and second mates had to manage a crew that was poorly paid and fed and lived in squalor on the filthy, fetid ships. Most of the crew were the dregs of society—renegades, castaways, criminals—though there were some men (usually young) of better quality who had a romantic yearning for adventure. The sailors were often badly treated, whipped, or placed in irons. They suffered a high death rate and were sometimes mutinous. Hugh Thomas, in his magisterial *The Slave Trade*, suggests that in the international trade one insurrection occurred for every eight to ten slave trips. Most of these mutinies were led by the crew, but some slave-led revolts were successful, especially if the slave ships were still near the African coast.

The masculine world of the officers and crew was crude. From the captain on down, the men filled their speech with curses and profanity, and the seamen on the slave ships treated the slaves as harshly as the officers did. The sailors were, as Captain Newton observed, "indifferent to the sufferings of their fellow-creatures."

The slaves were subjected to many indignities before, during, and after the Middle Passage, as the trip across the Atlantic from Africa to the Americas became known. They were inspected in the barracoons before they were sold; many of the larger slave ships had a doctor on board, who also minutely examined the slaves. They were often kept naked for the entire voyage, and the examinations of the women and girls were erotic. Men and boys were also scrutinized by traders, doctors, and purchasers. A guide for plantation owners suggested that slave penises be carefully examined, for if they were "underdeveloped or misshapen" they would be "bad for procreation."

Mortality rates among these captured Africans on the slave ships were high because of disease, inadequate food and water, crowded living conditions, and mistreatment. The abolitionist Thomas Clarkson, studying twenty voyages, calculated that 26 percent of the slaves died en route. The English Privy Council in 1789 estimated the average mortality during the Middle Passage at 12.5 percent. To that figure the Privy Council added a death toll of 4.5 percent for slaves in harbors before they were sold, and 33 percent who died during "seasoning"—the period of acclimation to the new environment. In total, then, half the slaves died in the time between leaving their homes and beginning work in the New World. These numbers confirm the extreme suffering endured by the African captives.

Slaves on the ships received too little food and water, and they lived in what can only be called inhuman conditions. The Reverend Pascoe C. Hill gives this account of the crowding of slaves on the *Progresso*, captured by the British navy in 1842: The slave deck was 36 feet long, 21 feet wide, and 3½ feet high, with 447 slaves packed into this space. The air was foul, for the naked slaves were lying in feces and urine. One night when a storm kept the slaves below deck, 54 of them died. Reports of the terrible conditions described by Reverend Hill were common. Slaves were constantly ill and dying on the international voyages. They had almost no fresh air in their quarters, and far too little was done to clean their holds. Some captains had the slave areas swabbed with vinegar water every few days, but that did little to stop the spread of disease, including the dread smallpox and the ever-present diarrhea.

Continual cries and lamentations could be heard from the sick and dying slaves. In addition to the terrible living conditions, they were often brutally beaten. Reverend Hill recorded what happened to slaves caught stealing water: "the culprits were 'seized up' with small cords to the forerigging, and received from fifteen to twenty lashes each from a rope's end; a Spaniard, an Englishman, and a strong negro relieving each other in the task."

Punishment for slaves who revolted was much harsher. In 1844 after an unsuccessful mutiny on the *Kentucky*, forty-six men and one woman were executed. Before they were killed "they were . . . chained two together and, when they were hanged, a rope was put around their necks and they were drawn up to the yardarm, clear of the sail. This did not kill them, but only choked or strangled them; they were then shot in the breast, and the bodies thrown overboard."

Captain Amasa Delano, a New Englander, wrote an account of the mutiny on the Spanish slave ship *Tryal* off the South American coast, an incident used by Herman Melville as the basis for his story "Benito Cereno." The mutineers were captured, and Delano quoted the official documents detailing their fate. The leaders were dragged "at the tail of a beast of burden, as far as the gibbet." After their execution, their heads were cut off and "fixed on a pole." The slave women and children on the ship were forced to watch the executions. Some rebellious slaves who had not been leaders of the mutiny were sent to prison.

For good reason then, most of the voyages were without uprisings. The usual practice was to separate men and women slaves to prevent sexual activity among them. On some voyages women were allowed to spend considerable time on deck, with the men contained below, because it was said that black women would "do what they could to urge the men to assert themselves and attack the crew." Having the women on the open deck with the slave men locked below also assured that the women and girls were available for sexual abuse by the officers and crew. According to one observer, by the time the slave ship left the African coast it "became half bedlam and half brothel."

About 1770 an officer on a French slave ship mistreated a pretty black woman, broke two of her teeth, and so terrorized her that when she arrived in Santo Domingo she had to be sold for an extremely low price. She died within two weeks. On transport ships and on land, slaves, both men and women, were at times tortured by sadists.

Captain Yves Armés, writing about an English ship off the West African coast, noted that the crew provided themselves with slave women—"*la coutume entre eux [est] d'avoir chacun leur femme*" (it is the custom for each one to have his own wife). The wives were temporary. Other voyages, other "wives."

A few captains sought to restrain their crews and protect the slave women and girls. Captain John Newton recalled one incident of his slaving days: "In the afternoon, while we were off the deck, William Cooney seduced a woman slave down into the room and lay with her brutelike, in view of the whole quarter deck, for which I put him in irons." Newton's action was not typical. Most captains allowed sex with slaves as a way of controlling the men under their command.

Olaudah Equiano, when a slave in the West Indies, was highly regarded by a Quaker merchant master, who gave him considerable responsibility. Equiano, a careful observer, wrote: "I was often a witness to cruelties of every kind, which were exercised on my unhappy fellow slaves. I used frequently to have different cargoes of new negroes in my care for sale; and it was almost a constant practice with our clerks, and other whites, to commit violent depredations on the chastity of the female slaves, and to these atrocities I was, though with reluctance, obliged to submit at all times, being unable to help them." John S. Jacobs addressed this male slave frustration when he wrote: "A slave's wife or daughter may be insulted before his eyes with impunity. He himself may be called on to torture them, and dare not refuse. To raise his hand in their defence is death by the law. He must bear all things and resist nothing."

Equiano spoke boldly about the treatment of young female slaves on domestic trips: "When we have had some of these slaves on board my master's vessels to carry them to other islands, or to America, I have known our mates commit these acts most shamefully, to the disgrace not of christians only, but of men. I have even known them gratify their brutal passion with females not ten years old. . . ."

Men and boy slaves were probably used sexually by some of the whites on international and domestic slave ships. Homosexual activity was common in the masculine world of sailors at sea. Herman Melville in 1843 signed on as a seaman on the frigate *United States* and used his experiences in writing the autobiographical fiction *White-Jacket*, published in 1850. What Melville had to say about homosexuality on a military ship may also be applied to commercial and slave ships: "Like pears closely packed, the crowded crew mutually decay through close contact, and every plague-spot is contagious. Still more, from

Olaudah Equiano

this same close confinement—so far as it affects the common sailors—arise other evils, so direful that they will hardly bear even so much as an allusion. What too many seamen are when ashore is very well known, but what some of them become when completely cut off from shore indulgences can hardly be imagined by landsmen. The sins for which the cities of the plain were overthrown still linger in some of these wooden-walled Gomorrahs of the deep. More than once complaints were made at the mast in the *Neversink*, from which the deck officer would turn away in loathing, refuse to hear them, and command the complainant out of his sight."

...*A*s of January 1, 1808, slaves could no longer be imported into the United States, but domestic sales and interstate transportation were allowed. The captains on U.S. domestic slave ship voyages before and after 1808 were in complete charge and typically had no interest in treating slaves humanely. On most of the U.S. ships, too, sailors were unconcerned with the suffering of slaves. The voyages were shorter than the now illegal ones from Africa to the United States, and for that reason living conditions did not deteriorate so dreadfully, but disease, including smallpox, remained a threat. Mutinies and plans for revolt continued, though on a more limited scale.

Domestic slave ships also cruised in Cuban waters. In 1817 an Anglo-Spanish treaty banned the importation of slaves from Africa into Cuba, but slavery remained legal there. In 1839 the *Amistad* was sailing between two ports in Cuba, illegally carrying fifty-three slaves just arrived from Africa. During that voyage the slaves, led by Cinqué, revolted. Cinqué reported that the captain was "very cruel" and beat slaves "severely." Sailors on the ship also participated in the whippings. As in the international voyages, slaves were punished for stealing water, and they were poorly fed—a day's rations consisted of one plantain, two potatoes, and half a cup of water. Celestino, the cook, once slapped Cinqué with a plantain, and it was Celestino who precipitated the mutiny. He told Cinqué that at the end of the voyage the slaves would be murdered by the Spaniards who would slit their throats, "chop their bodies into pieces, salt them down, and eat them as dried meat." Fearful of his fate and that of his fellow prisoners, Cinqué found a nail which he used to free himself and his chained compatriots. He had told his fellow captives in council: "If we do nothing we be killed. We may as well die in trying to be free as to be killed and eaten."

The slaves found sugar-cane knives for weapons and re-

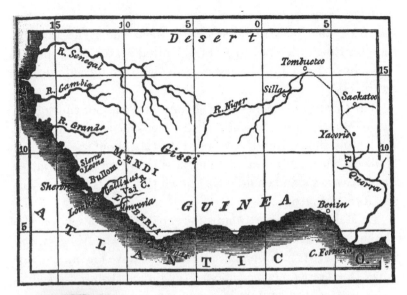

According to the entry on Cinqué in John W. Barber's *A History of the Amistad Captives* (1840), the leader of the mutiny was born in Men-di country. "His mother is dead, and he lives with his father. He has a wife and three children, one son and two daughters. . . . He is a planter of rice, and never owned or sold slaves. He was seized by four men, when traveling in the road, and his right hand tied to his neck. Ma-ya-gi-la-lo sold him to Ba-ma-dzha, son of Shaka, king of Gen-du-ma, in the Vai country. Bamadzha carried him to Lomboko and sold him to a Spaniard."

volted during the night while a storm raged. They killed the captain and the hated cook Celestino. Two crewmen tried to swim ashore and were apparently drowned. The owners of the slaves, José Ruiz and Pedro Montes, who were aboard the

Amistad, were spared. Montes was ordered to sail the ship to Africa, but instead he steered it near the Bahamas and then northward to the coast of the United States. He hoped to be stopped by a pro-slavery captain who would subdue the mutineers.

The *Creole* mutineers may well have heard about the duplicity of Montes, for accounts of the *Amistad* revolt appeared widely and slaves would have heard the talk about the incident. Madison Washington was in Canada when the *Amistad* matter was in the news and could have known the details of the revolt and its aftermath.

In Melville's story "Benito Cereno," based loosely on the Yankee captain Amasa Delano's *A Narrative of Voyages and Travels* . . . (1817), Babo and several other slave mutineers convince Delano, who comes aboard the hijacked ship, that all is normal—that the captain is in command and that the blacks are slaves. The naive Yankee captain is deceived until almost the end of the story. Once he learns what has really happened, he shows himself to be unconcerned about the slaves' desire for freedom. The rescued Spanish captain is shown to be cruel rather than benign. In fact, after the Americans had put down the mutiny, Delano had to restrain the Spanish captain from stabbing one of the slaves. The mutineers were saved only temporarily, of course, for the Spanish authorities later executed many of them and jailed others.

. . . Solomon Northup planned a slave revolt aboard the *Orleans* on its Richmond–New Orleans trip in 1841, just months before Madison Washington and the slaves on the *Creole* began the same journey. The *Orleans* was loaded with tobacco and forty slaves, less than one-third the number of slaves on the *Creole*. In *Twelve Years a Slave*, Northup offers glimpses of slave life on the *Orleans* and describes his plans for a mutiny that was unfortunately aborted. His account may provide clues to the revolt on the *Creole*.

Birch, the slave trader to whom the free Northup was sold illegally, purchased slaves along the way from Washington, D.C., to Norfolk, Virginia, and Northup in his narrative characterized and wrote brief histories of many of them. After he was drugged and sold to Birch, he began to evaluate the slaves around him. He was intent upon freeing himself, and he especially needed to decide which slaves could be trusted. Slaves with similar stories and histories must have been on the *Creole* with Madison Washington, but unfortunately their stories were not recorded. It seems certain that Washington studied his fellow slaves on the *Creole* as Northup did on the *Orleans*, trying to decide which ones might join him in revolt.

Of Northup's fellow slaves, one named Clemens Ray, from Washington, D.C., had worked as a hack driver for a livery stable. He was an intelligent man who understood what his life would be like once he was sold in New Orleans, and he was "overwhelmed with grief." Northup must have realized early on that Ray could not be roused to rebel.

Another, John Williams, was from Virginia. Birch had received him as payment for a debt. Williams kept hoping that he would be redeemed and not taken south, and eventually he was returned. Since it was possible that Williams might be returning to Virginia, Northup could not rely on him as a coconspirator.

Randall was a ten-year-old child who played about in the slave pen. He would at times call for his mother Eliza, but when not thinking of her he would amuse the adult slaves. He was too young to be a part of a mutiny.

Randall's mother, Eliza, and his half-sister Emily were brought into the slave pen the night before the slaves were moved to Richmond. Eliza had been the mistress of a wealthy planter who had left his wife and daughter and built a house for Eliza. He lived with her for nine years and was the father of Emily. His white daughter was the legal owner of Eliza, but she found the sight of Eliza "odious" and determined to sell her and her children.

Eliza and Emily were beautifully dressed; they had lived in ease and comfort, with servants, and their attitudes were different from those of uneducated slaves. Eliza was dressed in silks, with rings on her fingers, and she wore gold earrings. Emily was seven or eight years old. She had a "light complexion" and "a face of admirable beauty." As we have seen, Freeman expected to sell her for a high price.

Eliza was filled with lamentations about the fate of her children and her own fate. She was "weeping bitterly." She had been tricked the day she arrived at the slave pen: she was brought into Washington under the pretense that she and Emily would receive the papers showing they had been set free. Instead they were sold to Birch. Eliza was too distressed about her betrayal to be of any help in a revolt. In fact she could not survive as a Louisiana slave and did not live long in this new captivity.

At Goodin's slave pen in Richmond, Northup was handcuffed to Robert, a stout, yellow, melancholy man. Like Northup, Robert was born free. He had lived in Cincinnati with his wife and two children. He had gone to Fredericksburg, Virginia, to do some work, had been seized, and was being illegally sold. Robert would be a possible mutineer.

The night of Eliza's arrival, Robert, Clem, Eliza and her two children, and Northup, along with four others, all from the same plantation, slept in one of the small houses in the pen. Northup characterized those four, also bound for sale by Freeman in New Orleans.

David and Caroline, mulattoes, "dreaded the thought of being put into the cane and cotton fields; but their greatest source of anxiety was the apprehension of being separated." Northup must have found them too self-centered to be considered as possible mutineers.

Mary was tall and lithe and jet black. Northup said she "was listless and apparently indifferent. Like many of her class, she scarcely knew there was such a word as freedom. Brought up in the ignorance of a brute, she possessed but little more than a brute's intelligence. She was one of those, and there are very many, who fear nothing but their master's lash, and know no further duty than to obey his voice." She would not revolt.*

Lethe was the last of the four new arrivals. She looked more Indian than negroid. Northup wrote of her: "She had sharp and spiteful eyes, and continually gave utterance to the language of hatred and revenge. Her husband had been sold. . . . An exchange of masters, she was sure, could not be for the worse. . . . Pointing to the scars upon her face, the desperate creature wished that she might see the day when she could wipe them off in some man's blood!" Her name is ironic (perhaps fictitious), for she could not forget the horrors of her life in slavery. She could have been trusted only so far, for the urge for revenge was too strong for her to work with a group seeking freedom.

*Northup's attitude toward Mary and other slaves who had been brutalized and traumatized by slavery has been questioned recently by Walter Johnson, author of *Soul by Soul*, an excellent study of life inside the antebellum slave market. Johnson calls Northup "a deeply prejudiced person, certain of his own rectitude, suspicious and disdainful of most of his fellow slaves." Johnson seems to be unwilling to allow Northup, born a free man, to view slaves from his outsider position. Isn't it possible that Northup, from his perspective, offers realistic portraits of the slaves he met? Johnson admits that behind Northup's "disparaging descriptions" is the question: "who could be trusted?" When he was considering a mutiny, Northup certainly had to decide that question.

The day after departing from Richmond, the *Orleans* stopped in Norfolk to take aboard four more slaves. Northup wrote about them:

Frederick and Henry were both born slaves. Frederick was eighteen and Henry a few years older. They had been house servants in Norfolk. They were not involved in planning the mutiny, perhaps because they were considered too closely tied to the white world.

Northup's comments on Maria are worth quoting in full: she "was a rather genteel looking colored girl, with a faultless form, but ignorant and extremely vain. The idea of going to New Orleans was pleasing to her. She entertained an extravagantly high opinion of her own attractions. Assuming a haughty mien, she declared to her companions, that immediately on her arrival in New Orleans, she had no doubt, some wealthy single gentleman of good taste would purchase her at once!" The role of concubine was one she desired. Most of the slave narratives, when mentioning concubinage, make it clear that slave women often resisted. Here, apparently, one attractive woman had decided that being a mistress was better than working in the fields. The vain Maria, though, was not one who could be trusted in a mutiny.

The slave in this new group who engaged Northup's special attention was Arthur, who was struggling as he was placed on the ship. He was shouting that he was being mistreated and should be released. Northup found that Arthur was a free man, a longtime resident of Norfolk who had worked as a mason. He was attacked by a gang, overpowered, severely beaten, and confined in a slave pen. "For a time," Northup wrote, "he continued his protestations, and was altogether irreconcilable. At length, however, he became silent. He sank into a gloomy and thoughtful mood, and appeared to be counseling with himself.

There was in the man's determined face, something that suggested the thought of desperation." Northup recognized
Arthur as a prospective mutineer.

Once aboard the *Orleans*, Northup began to study his new
environment. His small knife was not taken from him, and he
must have realized that security on the ship was lax. The crew
was headed by a captain whose name Northup could not remember when he wrote his narrative but who has since been
identified as Mr. Wickham. Northup characterized him as a
small and genteel man who appeared to be "the personification
of courage." Northup gives no examples to illustrate the captain's bravery; perhaps he saw Wickham as a worthy opponent
once the mutiny began. The rest of the crew consisted of the
mate Biddee, a cook, and six sailors. Apparently there was no
guard on board, and the captain and mate undoubtedly took
those duties. The slaves had been handcuffed until the ship left
Norfolk, after which the cuffs were removed and the slaves allowed to remain on deck during the day. When they were free of
the cuffs it would have been much easier for them to revolt.
Northup made no references to whippings or to other cruelties
to slaves during the voyage.

Robert was named waiter for the captain, and Northup became head cook for the slaves. He was given the title of steward
and was assigned three assistants—Jim, Cuffee, and Jenny. Jim
and Cuffee boiled the bacon (salt pork) and baked the hoecakes
(a thin bread of cornmeal and water originally baked on a hoe
in the fields). Jenny made coffee by scorching cornmeal in a
kettle, adding water, boiling the dark liquid, and sweetening it
with molasses.

Northup observed that "Jim and Cuffee were very demure
and attentive to business, somewhat inflated with their situa-
tions as second cooks, and without doubt feeling that there was

a great responsibility resting on them." Northup would certainly not have whispered to them about the possibility of a mutiny.

The slaves were fed twice a day, at ten in the morning and five in the afternoon. Solomon stood at a table and gave each slave a hoecake and a slice of bacon. The slaves had no knives or forks and ate with their fingers. Each slave had a cup and filled it with "coffee." Both meals were exactly the same. At night the slaves "were driven into the hold," which was then secured with a covering.

The first night at sea the *Orleans* was enveloped in a heavy storm, and many of the slaves were seasick, making their hold "loathsome and disgusting," just as the slave quarters in the international trade ships were. Northup gives no indication that the hold was cleaned the next day. There were no bunks for the slaves; they slept on boxes or spread a blanket anywhere they could find a space on the floor.

The voyage was uneventful until the *Orleans* was in sight of Hole-in-the-Wall on the island of Abaco in the Bahamas. There the winds died, and the ship was stilled for three days. On the evening of the first day, Northup and Arthur in the bow of the *Orleans* began to talk about their misfortunes and what the future held for them. They agreed that death was better than life on a cotton or cane plantation. They began to talk of a mutiny and of sailing the ship to New York. They seemingly did not know that the British would free them once they reached Abaco. The two plotted, adopting plans, but whom could they trust? They decided to approach Robert, who they found was willing to join the revolt. All three were free men sold illegally into slavery. They felt it was not safe to approach the slaves on the ship, for they were, as Northup wrote, "brought up in fear and ignorance."

As the three worked on their plans, they found that a major

problem was how to get out of the locked hold at night. Northup noticed a small, overturned boat on the bow of the *Orleans*. He decided to crawl under it after supper and hope not to be missed as the slaves were moved into the hold. The plan worked; he spent the night in hiding and then mingled with his fellow slaves when they were allowed to come out the next day. The three planners aimed to hide under the overturned boat the night of the intended mutiny.

Since Robert was the waiter taking meals into the cabin shared by the captain and mate, he knew the location of their bunks and had also observed that two pistols and a cutlass were always on a table in the cabin. The cook slept in the galley, and the sailors were on the forecastle or in hammocks in the rigging.

Arthur and Northup were to steal out from their hiding place into the cabin where the captain and mate were sleeping, and kill them. Robert, with club in hand, was to stand at the door leading from the deck to the cabin and hold off the sailors should they be alarmed. Northup is vague about how the crew members were to be treated. Perhaps all were to be killed. If the mutiny did not go well, the plan was to call up the slaves in the hold and in the confusion gain control of the ship.

Before the mutiny could be carried out, Robert became ill with smallpox. Just when he had become infected is not known; the incubation period is usually ten to twelve days, but extremes from five to thirty-one days have been reported. Smallpox was often spread on international slave ships, causing a great many deaths. On the *Orleans* smallpox caused panic, and the captain ordered lime scattered in the hold—to no avail, of course. Later, in New Orleans, many of the slaves on the ship, including Northup, did develop smallpox.

The planned mutiny never happened. In his narrative, Northup rather halfheartedly declares that he thanked God the plan had been aborted without the taking of human lives.

Robert died on May 20, 1841, and was buried at sea. The *Orleans* reached New Orleans four days later.

In New Orleans, with the help of an English-born sailor, Northup was able to mail a letter about his kidnapping to Henry B. Northup, a white New York attorney who he claimed was "a relative of the family." But he could not then be traced and was to spend the next twelve years in captivity before being released and returned to his family in New York.

Later in the same year, on the *Creole*, Madison Washington and eighteen other slaves staged a revolt to gain their freedom. Washington had been free for a short time in Canada, and some of his followers may have been runaways to the North who had then been captured by bounty hunters and returned to Virginia for sale. Some may have been kidnapped free men or women. They were desperate and determined. Many of the more than one hundred other slaves on that ship must have been traumatized by the brutality of their treatment in slavery and could not be counted on for help in a mutiny. They were living without hope of taking control of their lives. In secret sessions between slaves who trusted one another, the revolt on the *Creole* was planned. It was not to be foiled by disease or betrayal.

V

The Mutiny on the Creole

THE *CREOLE* LAY at the Richmond dock for several days
in late October 1841 as slaves were brought in and supplies
loaded. Tobacco in boxes was brought aboard and stacked to
form a partition between the spaces in the hold allotted to men
and women slaves.

At midnight on October 25 the *Creole*, owned by Johnson &
Eperson of Richmond, Virginia, left the dock. She was a new
ship, having been built twelve or fourteen months earlier, and
she was insured for $16,000. The captain was Robert Ensor,
from Richmond. He obviously did not expect trouble from the
slaves during the voyage, for his wife, four-year-old daughter,
and fifteen-year-old niece were aboard. The ship carried 135 or
more slaves—there was a discrepancy between the number of
slaves listed in the ship's log and the number given in the New
Orleans Protest. Perhaps the *Creole* officers were poor at arith-
metic and kept miscounting slaves. More likely the *Creole* was
carrying some kidnapped free blacks who would not have been
in the official count. The *Orleans* that same year, as Solomon
Northup wrote, carried three kidnapped free black men.

John Hope Franklin and Loren Schweninger, in *Runaway
Slaves*, write that "economic, political, and societal pressures"
pushed "free persons of color back into slavery." They explain,

"Most lived on the margins of the southern economy, especially in the Upper South, with its large free black population, working as laborers, ditchdiggers, woodchoppers, dockhands, servants, porters, seamstresses, laundresses, carters, and at other humble tasks. . . . They were vulnerable to kidnappers and traders who sought a profit in human flesh."

It is also possible that the *Creole* was transporting some blacks from Africa who had been smuggled into the United States. Despite the official prohibition on importation, illegal trafficking in slaves did occur in several parts of the Americas. As noted, the slaves on the *Amistad* were Africans illegally brought into Cuba. We do not know that illegal Africans from Africa were on the *Creole*, but we do know that the ship's log and the Protests (the sworn declarations) in Nassau and New Orleans are incomplete and conceal many facts about happenings on the *Creole*.

As the *Creole* sailed down the James River, Captain Ensor went ashore several times to return with slaves, including three or four belonging to Thomas McCargo. Ensor's aggressive search for slaves to transport to Louisiana suggests that in addition to his regular salary as captain, he received an extra sum for each slave being transported. Nothing in the records indicates that he objected to trafficking in slaves. He was undoubtedly a traditional slave-ship captain and treated slaves harshly and cruelly.

The captain may have been allowed to trade in slaves for himself. On a French slaver in 1731, Captain Mary had permission, as Robert Harms writes in *The Diligent*, to acquire a certain number of slaves on his own account. He bought more than had been agreed upon, making it possible to earn more when the slaves were sold. When one of his slaves died during the voyage, he "recorded the death as that of a slave belonging

The *Creole* was somewhat smaller than this three-masted brig of two hundred tons used to transport slaves. The *Creole* had a tonnage of 157 and 25/95, and was probably two-masted.

to the *Diligent's* outfitters." Slave captains could be as unscrupulous as slave traders.

The *Creole*, with her load of slaves and tobacco—planted, harvested, and manufactured by slaves—moved out to sea. The captain and the crew believed that the journey would be peaceful, and as on the *Orleans* earlier that year, the slaves were neither chained nor restrained. They could move around at will, though they were segregated at night into men's and women's quarters. For some reason Washington, known to have been a runaway and of exceptional strength, was not kept in chains. There must have been other slaves on board who had strong feelings against the whites who enslaved them, and who might have been expected to be "troublemakers," but they also were not in chains. The captain, the crew, and the guards were apparently so confident of a quiet voyage that they were oblivious to the whisperings and plotting going on among the slaves.

From the routine described by Solomon Northup and from a close reading—sometimes between the lines—of the official documents concerning the mutiny, we can establish some of what occurred during the early days of the trip.

Madison Washington, like Solomon Northup on the *Orleans*, was named head cook for the slaves. He would have had several assistants, and he would have supervised the cooking of the salt pork and salt beef and the boiling of the coffee made from parched grain. On the *Orleans* the slaves had been given corn pone, but undoubtedly because of the greater number of slaves on the *Creole*, bread was not being baked; instead prepared hardtack (unleavened bread in hard wafers) was used. Twice a day, at 10 a.m. and 5 p.m., Washington would likely have stood at a serving table and given each slave a slice of boiled meat on a piece of hardtack. An assistant would have served a cup of "coffee" to each slave.

From his position as head cook, Washington had a unique vantage point. He had to be on deck most of the day supervising his cooks, where he could have observed and talked with the officers and sailors. He would have spoken to each slave as he gave them food. He could have quietly noted the routines established by the crew and officers and especially the weaknesses in the guard system.

Washington and his colleagues who were recruiting trustworthy participants for a revolt must have been studying the personalities of the officers, crew, guards, and slaves on the ship. After the mutiny, no slave was allowed to give official—or even unofficial—testimony; so we have no direct proof of how brutal or unjust the captain was in his treatment of the slaves. A Virginia captain of a slave ship, however, was likely to be harsh. During the mutiny the slaves wanted him dead, which suggests that he was not humane in his treatment of them. Madison Washington would have known just how brutal or unjust the mates, crew, and guards were. The first and second mates were authority figures, and in the early stages of the revolt the slaves felt they needed to be killed. Members of the crew who did not attempt to fight the slaves were in little danger, and they were later protected by Washington. The slaves, though, took pleasure in killing John R. Hewell, McCargo's agent and guard, a sure sign of his brutality, as would be expected of someone in his position, working as he did for a man who fits the classic mold of an unscrupulous slave trader. Merritt, assigned to guard over all the slaves, and having taken that position to gain free passage to New Orleans, was in particular danger during the revolt simply because of his position.

Washington had firsthand knowledge of the crowded, unsanitary conditions on the ship. He knew, though the official record is unclear, just how many slaves were on the *Creole*. He knew, though we do not, the size of their quarters and their sleeping arrangements. We assume the slaves spread their blankets on the deck or on crude wooden bunks.

Washington would have known, too, just how poorly the slaves were fed, for he could easily see what William Devereux, the free black cook, was preparing for the officers, the crew, Ensor's family, and the guards. Washington and his followers would have observed that the captain, mates, and guards were complacent and incompetent, that they did not expect the slaves to turn on them and therefore did not think it necessary to keep them in chains or lock them in the hold at night. They would have known, too, that the crew had not searched the slaves when they boarded the *Creole*, and therefore did not know if knives and guns were being smuggled on board. The captain, or the mates acting on his orders, early on brought six women from the female slave quarters, supposedly for housekeeping and maid duties in the cabin. They were not returned to the female quarters at night. As Walter Johnson suggested in *Soul by Soul*, these females likely served the sexual needs of the white males. On the international slave ships and in the slave pens, slave women and girls were made into "wives." Slave men and boys on the *Creole* may have been forced or bribed into homosexual acts. Madison Washington would have known about the various sexual activities on the ship and used this knowledge as he and others were planning to revolt.

From the official records, we know the identity of two of the "wives": Rachel Glover, about thirty, and Mary, a mulatto girl about thirteen years old. Mary was undoubtedly, in Freeman's terms, an "extra fancy piece" as Emily was, and McCargo could have had Freeman sell her for a high price. Rachel's five-year-old son was kept with the slave women in the hold, not in the cabin with her. His presence would have interfered with her duties as a temporary wife for the white men.

Owners and captains of domestic slave ships kept men and women slaves apart to prevent, they insisted, the spread of venereal disease. The irony is that the officers, sailors, and guards who called at many ports and visited their bordellos were more likely than blacks to be infected with such disease.

The slave men and women on the *Creole*, separated specifically to prevent sexual activity between them, were surely angry and frustrated when they boarded the ship and further incensed when white men turned the six "maids" into "wives." Madison Washington had failed to rescue his wife, and he must have been particularly distraught and sexually frustrated at never seeing her again, never having her again as his wife.

The official records ignore the conditions on the *Creole*, but the slaves, whether angry, defiant, frustrated, or depressed almost to the point of inertia, were acutely aware of the hopelessness of their situation. They carried within themselves the cruelty of their past, and they knew their lives were likely to be worse after they were sold in New Orleans. Several were ready to risk their lives to gain their freedom. Had Madison Washington and the other slaves been interviewed after the revolt, they would have had many stories, some horrible, to tell about their lives in slavery, about their days on the *Creole*, and about their aspirations for freedom. As Northup did, they could have given character sketches of people they had previously known and of the officers, crew, and guards on the *Creole*. They also could have given details of the characters and opinions of their fellow slaves on the ship.

The mutiny was likely planned entirely by the slaves themselves. After the *Creole* finally reached New Orleans, stories circulated that a minister in Virginia had helped with the planning of the revolt, but that seems to be a rumor many Southerners wanted to hear. Southern upholders of the peculiar institution of slavery wished to believe that slaves were not clever enough to plan and carry out a mutiny by themselves.

. . . *W*hen the revolt began, Elijah Morris fired his gun at Gifford, grazing the back of his head. The first mate then ran to the cabin shouting, "There's a mutiny on deck! I've been shot." How did the slaves happen to have a gun? Was it brought aboard in one of their packs? Possibly, because the testimony at the insurance trials indicates that the slaves and their belongings were not examined before they boarded the *Creole*. Gifford nonchalantly testified at the insurance trials: "If any pistols or weapons of any kind had been seen in possession of the negroes, they would not have been permitted to retain them." Was the gun taken from a stateroom, as Robert had planned to do on the *Orleans*? The officers on the *Creole* did not care to talk about how the slaves on the ship gained possession of the gun.

The captain and all the others in the staterooms were awakened. Seventeen male slaves rushed out of the hold to join Madison Washington and Elijah Morris and surrounded the cabin. Merritt blew out the lamp he was holding. The *Creole* was now in darkness except for the lantern on the bow. For the next few hours the darkness added to the danger and fear on deck, in the passageways, and in the staterooms. Shouts from blacks and whites filled the air.

At first Merritt was not able to escape. Slaves caught him, and one shouted, "That is he; kill him by God." It would appear that in the whispered sessions of male slaves in the hold, the insurrectionists had decided that the officers and guards on the *Creole* had to be killed in order to intimidate the other crew members if the slaves were to be successful in their desperate attempt for freedom. Solomon Northup's plans for the mutiny on the *Orleans* had been similar: the captain and mate were to be killed. On the *Creole* the easygoing officers and sailors had left handspikes around on deck; one slave attempted to hit Merritt with one of the heavy bars, missed, and struck one of the mutineers.

Hewell, asleep in his berth, was aroused by the shouts and commotion. He had no gun in his stateroom and rushed into Stevens's stateroom to get the one musket on board. He then went topside to confront the mutineers. He fired at them, but the musket, with powder but no shot in it, was useless—another indication that the guards' incompetence had worked in the slaves' favor once again. The mutineers grabbed the musket from Hewell, who then picked up a handspike. In the darkness, the black men mistook the heavy bar for another musket and temporarily retreated.

Captain Ensor, with no musket or pistol at his disposal—something of an oversight on his part—grabbed a bowie knife and went on deck in an attempt to rally the seamen there. He

joined Hewell, who was now faced with several regrouped mutineers. In the fight that took place, the captain was stabbed
several times. One of the mutineers cried out: "Kill the son-of-
a-bitch, Kill him." The slaves pursued him into the starboard
scuppers, where he was stabbed several more times and beaten
with sticks of wood the slaves found on deck. Ensor was severely injured and bleeding profusely, but he was able to climb
into the maintop, where it was completely dark and where he
was temporarily safe.

Ben [the Blacksmith] Johnstone had seized the captain's
bowie knife and joined the battle against Hewell, who was soon
knocked down. Johnstone and Morris, who also had a knife,
stabbed Hewell at least twenty times. Johnstone and Morris
appear to have been the most bloodthirsty of the mutineers. We
do not know their stories, but they must have been treated brutally in the past and perhaps on the *Creole*. They may also have
been involved in the stabbing of the captain, but the record is
not clear on this point.

Hewell managed to escape to the stateroom he shared with
young McCargo. Hewell cried out prophetically, "I am a dead
man. The damned negroes have killed me." He managed to get
into McCargo's berth, and within half an hour he was dead.
Several slaves entered the stateroom to observe his death.

As the blacks began their search for white people on board,
lights came on in some of the staterooms. The blacks then
threw water through the skylights to extinguish the lamps.
Soon the only light was from the lanterns used by the searching
parties of blacks and the lantern on the bow.

Jacob Leitner, the Prussian serving as steward in exchange
for his passage to New Orleans; William Devereux, the free
black cook; and Lewis, Thomas McCargo's trusted slave who
was acting as steward, were all concealed in a single stateroom.
As the slaves began a search of the staterooms, they called out

that all in that room should come out or they would be killed immediately. Leitner emerged first, saying, "Here I am—do what you please." Devereux and Lewis came out next. The three were pleading for their lives, and all were spared. Although the nineteen rebellious slaves were using threatening language, it is clear that the officers and guards were in greatest danger. Madison Washington, holding a lighted lantern, was heard to say, "Where are the captain and the mate? These are the persons we want." In the confusion of the mutiny he did not know that the captain had been seriously injured and had climbed into the maintop.

While this was going on, another scene had been played out almost in slow motion. After the alarm was given and Hewell rushed from his stateroom, young McCargo rose from his berth, dressed slowly, and stayed where he was. The injured Hewell returned, climbed into McCargo's berth, and was followed by slaves. McCargo took out one of his two pistols from a case and fired at the blacks in his vicinity, but he hit no one. He then took the other pistol from the case, but it misfired. He had no ammunition, and he put the pistols back in their case before the slaves took him prisoner. Old Lewis begged, "Master Theo should not be killed." Elijah Morris and Ben Johnstone spared the boy's life.

Escaping slaves on land or on water had reason to fear the guard dogs of slave owners and those involved in the slave trade. In this revolt on the *Creole*, the captain's dog fought furiously and bit several slaves before being killed.

William Merritt made it into a stateroom and attempted to escape through a skylight, but it was being guarded by a slave and Merritt was unable to flee. He then crawled under the bedclothes in an empty berth, and two or three women slaves, the "maids" in the cabin, sat on him. They were crying and praying, and for a time Merritt was safe.

Gifford escaped to the maintop where he found the captain, who had been bleeding heavily and had fainted. Gifford then tied Ensor to the rigging to prevent him from falling.

Stevens, the second mate, was cautious during the fight. After a minor scuffle with the mutineers, he and Blinn Curtis, a seaman, retreated to a stateroom. The blacks had begun to search for Stevens, who heard one of them say, "The captain, the [first] mate, and Hewell are all dead, and now we'll have that long, tall son-of-a-bitch second mate." The slaves in that search party may have thought that three men had been killed, but it is just as likely they were spreading misinformation to frighten the second mate. The revolting slaves seem to have understood how to wage psychological warfare.

Stevens and Curtis could hear the slaves searching the staterooms, one by one. They came to the one occupied by Mrs. Ensor and the two children. Mrs. Ensor pleaded for the three not to be harmed, and one slave said, "Leave these alone for the last; we want the second mate, and the brig will be ours." Mrs. Ensor and the children were not harmed and were placed under guard.

When the slaves reached the cabin where Stevens and Curtis were hiding, a mutineer pointed the musket taken from Hewell—a musket now properly loaded—at Stevens. But the second mate turned away the muzzle, and he reported that one of the slaves was wounded by the shot. Stevens then escaped to the main deck, where a black struck him with a flagstaff and another stabbed him. Again he escaped and climbed to the foreroyal yard, joining the captain and first mate. The three were temporarily safe.

From his perch Stevens reported that he saw Hewell's body brought out on deck, and he observed the mutineers with a knife cutting off his head as near as possible. Johnstone then declared, "We will separate the old son of a bitch somehow."

Hewell's almost decapitated body was then cast overboard. No kind words about Hewell were recorded in any of the official documents about the *Creole* affair. Later Ben Johnstone remarked that he had sent some people to hell that night. When he used "people" he must have assumed that the captain was dead.

Throughout the official papers about the mutiny the blacks curse freely, but Hewell is the only white who curses, and in his case only once: after he knew he was dying he referred to "damned negroes." The first word in his quote was probably much stronger, and he undoubtedly said "niggers" instead of "Negroes." Sailors, known through the ages for their cursing, use language in the official mutiny documents appropriate for a Sunday school picnic. The speech of the black mutineers is not rendered in dialect. Indeed, except for the cursing, everyone on the *Creole* speaks standard English.

Blinn Curtis, in the stateroom after Stevens had escaped, fought with the mutineers. He received a cut over one eye from a blow from a handspike. He managed to get on deck and was planning to climb the rigging but was captured. He was not harmed in captivity.

Merritt, in the meantime, was hidden by the two or three frightened maids. Just why they were protecting him is not clear. If, as is likely, the six women servants were expected to provide sexual favors for the whites on board, it may be that he had treated them humanely and given them trinkets and special privileges. Whatever the reasons, the women became more afraid when they heard Ben Johnstone call out that those hiding Merritt would be killed. The women left, and Merritt hid himself under the mattress. He was soon found and heard this frightening shout, "Kill the son-of-a-bitch, don't spare him, and kill every white person on board, don't spare one." Ben Johnstone and Elijah Morris dragged him from the berth with their knives and handspikes ready. The slaves made room for him to fall. He hastily told his captors that he had once been mate on a ship and could navigate the *Creole* for them. Mary, the young slave assigned to the cabin, pleaded for his life.

Madison Washington then took Merritt into a stateroom for a conversation. Washington said he wanted the *Creole* taken to Liberia. It is not clear why he did not indicate he wanted the ship taken to Nassau, for he knew from living in Canada that the British had abolished slavery and would free the slaves once the ship docked in the Bahamas. It may be that he declared his wish to have the *Creole* taken into the Bahamas, but the whites giving testimony deliberately reported him saying that the slaves wanted to go to Liberia. Or it could be that Washington wanted no part of the Western civilization that had kept him enslaved.

Merritt told Washington that the *Creole* did not have enough water or provisions for such a long voyage. Other slaves urged that the ship be taken into a Bahamian port. Some of them knew that a year earlier an American ship had gone aground in the Bahamas and that the British had freed all the slaves aboard.

Merritt, using the chart, showed Washington and his other captors how he could navigate them into a port where they would be freed. The slaves agreed that they would spare his life if he would do so. But the nineteen mutineers knew that Merritt and the other captives would betray them if they had the opportunity. Merritt was placed under guard along with Devereux, Leitner, McCargo, Curtis, and the captain's wife and children. The slaves knew that several white men had climbed the rigging and would soon be taken prisoner.

By a little after 1 a.m. the revolt was over. Madison Washington and his followers were in control of the *Creole*.

. . . *A*fter the revolt the blacks, in control of the ship, continued their shouts and threats, but there were no more deaths or injuries. Madison Washington acted to protect all of those who were captured. The nineteen rebels knew who was not accounted for among the whites, but in the darkness they could not locate them in the rigging. Finally about 4:30 that morning Elijah Morris, with four or five other mutineers, spotted second mate Stevens on the foreroyal yard. Morris called out, "Come down, you damn son of a bitch, receive your message; that is the very one we want." Stevens started down slowly while the slaves cried out their "message" to him. On his way down Stevens asked why they wished to kill him. Morris replied, "Damn you, come down and receive your message." The message, of course, was to help steer the *Creole* to the Bahamas and freedom.

Once Stevens was on deck, he asked the mutineers for five minutes to talk, and he promised that if they would spare his life he would take them into a Bahamian port within three days. The response: "We will give you three days; if you don't we will throw you overboard, if not before."

Gifford came down from his perch, and Washington asked where the captain was. Gifford replied that the captain was tied in the maintop and asked permission to bring him down. One rebel shouted, "Damn him, let him stay there till daylight, and we will finish him then."

Once Gifford reached the poop deck, he began to talk to Washington and some of the other slaves. Washington told Gifford to take the *Creole* to Abaco, otherwise he would be tossed over the side.

Merritt was brought from the hold, and Gifford, Stevens, and Merritt were told to "put sail on the vessel," and they did so. Immediately the mutineers said it was too early, and they ordered the sail taken down. Gifford, seeing that no one was in charge, asked who was to be obeyed. Madison Washington, having played a dominant role in the mutiny, became the designated leader, with Elijah Morris, Ben Johnstone, and Dr. Ruffin as his lieutenants.

Gifford now told Stevens to take a bottle of water to the captain. As Stevens began the climb, Morris and Washington called to him: "Come down, you son-of-a-bitch," for they clearly would not allow Gifford to give orders. Stevens came down, Merritt consulted with a party of mutineers, and they allowed Stevens to take some water up to the injured captain. Not long afterward Stevens and one of the crew brought the captain down in a sling; he was placed on a mattress and locked in the forehold. His wife was allowed to join him to attend to his wounds. By this time it was 6 a.m.

Gifford's testimony in the Louisiana trials of slave owners against the companies that had written insurance on the slaves was explicit: once it was clear who was in charge on the *Creole*, the mutineers "kept strict orders over the rest of the negroes, exercising the same sway over the rest of the negroes that they did over the whites, threatening to whip them if they disobeyed their orders." What Gifford did not understand is that keeping order probably saved lives. Among the men and women slaves who did not take part in the revolt there were probably some who would have been especially bloodthirsty once the blacks were in charge. Also, the mutineers recognized the problem of treachery. After the revolt had begun, one slave named Andrew Jackson announced that he was afraid of the mutineers, and he climbed the rigging for safety.

Gifford testified that the nineteen mutineers took over the cabin as their headquarters. Leitner, the Prussian who was acting as assistant steward, reported that during the affray when Morris was threatening to kill all whites, he asked Morris if he were included in that death list. Morris said "No" and sent him into the afterhatch. Later, once the *Creole* was securely in their possession, the nineteen sent for him to ask where the liquor was kept.

When Leitner indicated its location, he was told to pass it out. He handed over "four bottles of brandy, a jug of whiskey, and a demijohn of Madeira wine." The nineteen, joined by some of the whites, drank all the brandy and most of the whiskey and wine, but they did not ask the other slaves to join them. The nineteen also called for apples and bread, not hardtack. The alcohol and better food had been available only to the whites on board.

Leitner also saw some of the nineteen open the trunks of "passengers." In the official testimony, Leitner, young McCargo, Hewell, and Merritt were referred to as "passengers." Leitner's account attempts to put the actions of the mutineers in the worst possible light: He saw them take $10.50 from Hewell's trunk. He observed them taking clothes out of other trunks, including the captain's. One slave had Leitner's watch, but it was returned to him, "the slave saying he thought it was the captain's." Leitner thought some of the slaves buffoonish, as he saw some of them "putting on the passengers' stockings, leaving the old ones in their places." The cabin was guarded at all times, he said, by one mutineer with a gun, another with a knife, and still another with a pistol.

The nineteen had good reason to distrust the whites on the *Creole*. When the whites testified in Nassau, at a time when it was thought the slaves might possibly be returned to officials of the United States, the names of the nineteen mutineers were specifically mentioned in connection with acts of violence. If these nineteen had been sent back to the United States, likely they would have been tried and several executed. Only the nineteen were mentioned as mutineers. It appears there was a conscious attempt not to implicate other blacks on board, thus saving them for sale in New Orleans.

Sexual activities between whites and blacks on the ship were not mentioned in the New Orleans Protest, but that document contained expressions of horror that some of the nineteen mutineers had expressed themselves sexually in the period just after the *Creole* was seized: "Some of the nineteen were hugging some of the female servants in the cabin; and one of them said he had picked out one of them for his wife, but none of the others had anything to do with the female servants." ·

About daybreak on November 8, 1841, the brig was steered for Nassau. The officers and crew were forbidden to speak among themselves, except when a slave guard was present. Dr. Ruffin had previously been to New Orleans and could tell if the *Creole* was being steered in the wrong direction. He could also read the compass—probably it was this skill that gave him the title "Doctor," which caused some confusion in the official documents, where he is sometimes identified as Dr. Ruffin and at other times as D. Ruffin. Dr. Ruffin could make certain that Merritt, Stevens, and Gifford were not secretly steering the ship toward New Orleans.

These three—Merritt, Stevens, and Gifford—were watched carefully. As noted in the New Orleans Protest, when Dr. Ruffin saw Merritt mark on the slate the heading he was taking, Ruffin "compelled him to rub out the words in writing, and make only figures and marks on the slate, for fear that Gifford and Merritt might communicate secretly by that means." Once, when Gifford spoke to Merritt about the reckoning, Morris told them that if they spoke to each other again they would be thrown over the side.

At first Stevens was not trusted by Washington and his men to be allowed to join Merritt and Gifford in bringing the *Creole* into Nassau, but Gifford requested that the captors allow

Stevens to come on deck to "take an observation of the sun." After that, Ben Johnstone, armed with a gun, said to Stevens: "You had better go below and stay there, or you will be thrown overboard, as there are a number of bad negroes on board."

Stevens did go below, joining the injured captain, his family, and other captives. After the grating over the lower deck had been fastened, Elijah Morris spoke to Stevens: "Mr. Stevens, I don't wish to see you hurt, but they talk strong in the cabin of heaving you over this night." Stevens then asked Morris to consult with Washington about protecting him.

The mood among the captors was erratic. The captain wanted more air and asked that the grating be removed. His request was granted, indicating that the mutineers wanted him to survive. Stevens was called back on deck and went about his duties as mate. About 1 p.m. on November 8, Stevens went into the cabin to get his dinner. One of the nineteen was sitting at the table, menacingly, with a gun under his arm, but Stevens made it safely through his meal. At 8 p.m. that same day, while walking on the quarterdeck, Stevens heard a gun fire and a ball whistle past him. Gifford then told him to climb the masthead to look for the Abaco light. While he was climbing, he heard one of the nineteen who was loading a gun say, "Make haste, be quick." Stevens made haste, and he was soon out of reach. The gun was not fired, and the slaves laughed. Some of the threats against Stevens were evidently idle, for purposes of intimidation. If so, they succeeded: he was not likely to take part in any plot to recapture the *Creole*.

Gifford, when cross-examined during the insurance trials, asserted that the white crew members were carefully watched by the nineteen and that there was absolutely no way the crew could have retaken the ship. Like Stevens, he was threatened and had given up hope of ever being on land again, "as the negroes declared as soon as they got near the land they would kill all the whites on board but the Frenchman and run the vessel ashore themselves."

Madison Washington was now separated from his wife by an expanse of ocean (we assume she was still alive in Virginia), hardly a joyous time for him. The author of the *Friend of Man* article about Washington, searching for a happy ending, or at least the possibility of one, writes: "Is he [Washington] still without his beloved wife? Remember it was Madison's visit 'aft among the women' that led to the first act of violence on the *Creole*. Might not his wife have been there among the women. Yes, and this grave *Creole* matter may prove to have been a part only of that grand game, in which the highest stake was the liberty of his dear wife. Will not some British abolitionists obtain for us the story from Madison's own lips?" As we show in the Appendix, several writers about the *Creole* incident wanted a happy ending, and they arranged for Washington's wife Susan to reappear after the revolt ended, with the two lovers reunited. There is no evidence to support such a conclusion. If his wife had been aboard the ship, Washington would have seen her when he was serving meals to his fellow captives.

At daybreak on November 9, 1841, the *Creole* came in sight of Nassau. Once the ship entered the harbor, Washington collected the knives and two pistols and threw most of them overboard. He kept in his possession one pistol and the musket. While the nineteen mutineers were not as heavily armed as before, it would have been useless for the crew to try to overcome them, though in the insurance trials the lawyers for the companies suggested they should have done so.

When the *Creole* was about one mile from the lighthouse, a black pilot with some of his crew came on board, and they mingled with the blacks. As the pilot was bringing the ship into harbor, a quarantine officer arrived in his boat, and Gifford jumped into it, explaining that a mutiny had taken place. He asked to be taken ashore and requested that the *Creole* be watched "to let them have no communication with the shore till he returned." He knew that once the slaves set foot in Nassau they were free.

Arriving in Nassau, Gifford hastened to see the American consul to request help in recapturing the slaves and preventing them from being freed by the British government.

The effort of Madison Washington and his compatriots to free themselves and a large number of their fellow slaves was now entering its final phase.

VI

The Creole *Slaves in Nassau*

FIRST MATE GIFFORD, assuming the responsibilities
of the badly injured captain of the *Creole*, on the morning of
November 9, 1841, rushed to see John F. Bacon, United States
consul, about the revolt on the ship. Once Gifford had explained the situation, the two men immediately called upon
Colonel Sir Francis Cockburn, governor of the Bahamas, re-
questing his assistance in preventing the slaves from escaping
and in securing the mutineers. We know Cockburn's immediate
reaction from Bacon's letter of November 30, 1841, to Daniel
Webster, then secretary of state in Washington. Bacon wrote
that Sir Francis "doubted whether he was authorized to interfere with them at all, but under the circumstances [the murder
that had occurred during the mutiny], felt inclined to comply
with my request." Gifford was examined by the governor and
his testimony taken down. Cockburn also asked Bacon to put
his request in writing, and that was done.

In light of his initial response and subsequent actions, it is
not likely that Cockburn was planning to allow Bacon, representing a government that allowed slavery, to reclaim slaves.
The British government had abolished slavery in the West Indies almost a decade earlier. Cockburn, however, did need to
appear to be making an impartial investigation.

After the interview with Cockburn, Bacon advised Gifford to board the *Creole* and "keep the colors set." Acting for the governor, the colonial secretary of the Bahamas, C. R. Nesbitt, wrote Bacon on November 9 that "his excellency has ordered a military party on board of the said brig," where Bacon soon "found the slaves very quiet." Bacon placed Gifford in command. At noon the Bahamian military party—twenty black soldiers with loaded muskets and fixed bayonets, a black corporal and a black sergeant, and a white officer—boarded the ship. Bacon then departed, taking with him the severely wounded Captain Ensor and two injured sailors.

Soon afterward, Bacon received a message to appear before the governor and his council, then in session. When he arrived, Bacon was told what actions were to be taken, and was presented with a written statement that was clear, to the point, and not to Bacon's liking:

"1st. That the courts of law here have no jurisdiction over the alleged offences.

"2d. But that as an information had been lodged before his excellency the Governor, charging the crime of murder to have been committed on board of the said vessel while on the high seas, it was expedient that the parties implicated in so grave a charge should not be allowed to go at large, and that an investigation ought therefore to be made into the charges, and examinations taken on oath, when it should appear that the original information was correct, and that a murder had actually been committed, that all the parties implicated in such a crime, or in any other acts of violence should be detained here until reference could be made to the Secretary of State [in London] to ascertain whether the parties detained should be delivered over to the American Government or not, and if not, how otherwise to be disposed of.

"3rd. That so soon as such examinations should be taken,

all the persons on board of the *Creole*, not implicated in any of the offences alleged to have been committed on board of that vessel, must be released from further restraint."

Bacon hoped to return all the mutineers to the United States for trial and almost certain execution for several of them, and to send the rest of the blacks on to New Orleans for the slave pens and eventual sale. He would seek ways to foil Cockburn and the British government.

Two magistrates and Bacon now went on board the *Creole* and began to take statements. The depositions continued Tuesday and Wednesday but were canceled on Thursday because of the illness of Captain Ensor. They resumed on Friday. The slaves were not questioned, therefore we know only a part of the story of the mutiny. The testimony of the whites on the *Creole* seems rehearsed and is often self-serving. Every person deposed followed Cockburn's wishes and named as many of the conspirators as they could, but they also seemed anxious not to implicate most of the slaves. They all insisted that the women slaves knew nothing about the plot, though this was probably not true.

The four leaders of the revolt—Madison Washington, Ben Johnstone, Dr. Ruffin, and Elijah Morris—were quickly identified, put in a longboat, tied, and guarded by a sentry. The other fifteen mutineers were identified during the interrogations and were also placed under guard.

The Bahamian military party mingled with the slaves and, according to the New Orleans Protest, "told the women they were free and persuaded them to remain on the island." One of the Nassau pilot's crew, according to that Protest, told a female slave he would claim her for his wife. The Americans swearing to the New Orleans Protest wanted to show that the Bahamian troops were sexually rapacious. Merritt, in his depositions in the Bahamas, reported that he saw on the day the slaves were liberated the British commanding officer "conversing with a colored female with his cloak around her." The implication is that the cloak was around both of them to hide sexual activity. Slave women over the centuries were certainly preyed upon by men of many nationalities and races, and Merritt's observation may well be true. The official documents about the mutiny, however, present the American whites on the *Creole* as nonsexual beings.

On the Wednesday after the *Creole* arrived in Nassau, the British Captain Fitzgerald put his arms around the thirteen-year-old Mary, who was assigned to the cabin, and remarked "how foolish they were, that they had not, when they rose, killed all the whites on board, and run the vessel ashore, and then they would all have been free, and there would have been no more trouble about it."

The signers of the New Orleans Protest made it clear that they were in unfriendly territory in Nassau, where support for the British decision to free slaves was overwhelming. There were, according to that account, "twelve or thirteen thousand negroes in the town of Nassau and vicinity, and about three or four thousand whites." There were five hundred soldiers on the island.

Bacon's argument that "slaves were as much a portion of the cargo as the tobacco" was offensive to the British officials. The pro-slavery views of the whites on the *Creole* were also unacceptable in the Bahamas. Gifford reported that he was recognized by both blacks and whites on the streets of Nassau, and they said of him, "There goes one of the damned pirates and slavers."

In spite of the odds against them, Bacon and Gifford had a secret plan to retake the *Creole* and send it on its way back to the United States. The bark *Louisa* and the brig *Congress*, both flying the flag of the United States, were then in Nassau harbor. Captain Woodside of the *Louisa* was brought into the plot. He was to gather members of his crew, his second mate, and four sailors from the *Congress*, arm them, board the *Creole*, and take over the ship from the Bahamian troops. The plan was to sail the liberated *Creole* to Indian Key, Florida, where they would find a U.S. vessel of war.

Bacon and Gifford tried to purchase guns in Nassau but were everywhere refused, for the population had sided with the slaves. From the *Louisa* and the *Congress* the American conspirators could gather only three muskets, three cutlasses, and a pair of horse pistols. The plotters were certainly no match for the well-armed troops guarding the *Creole*.

Nevertheless at 8 a.m. on Friday, November 12, this poorly conceived and laughably armed raid began. The small cache of arms was wrapped in an American flag and placed out of sight in the boarding boat. The party trying to retake the *Creole* was observed by a black Bahamian, who alerted the British officer on the *Creole*. That officer ordered the boarding party to "Keep off, or I will fire into you." Twenty-four troops were standing on the deck of the *Creole* "with loaded muskets and fixed bayonets" at the ready. Captain Woodside and his men, no more effective than young McCargo had been several nights earlier, withdrew.

In the New Orleans Protest the whites on the *Creole* asserted that "if there had been no interference on the part of the legal authorities of Nassau, the slaves might have been safely brought to New Orleans. It was that interference which prevented aid from being rendered by the American sailors in Nassau, and caused the loss of slaves to their owners." Had that boarding party been well armed, and had they succeeded in taking the ship, the action would likely have caused a major diplomatic confrontation between the British and United States governments.

The depositions of crew and passengers were to have resumed that Friday, but they were canceled without explana-
tion—most likely because of Captain Woodside's aborted
attempt to retake the *Creole*. Bacon wrote the governor at noon
that day: "On proceeding to go on board the brig *Creole*, with
the magistrates this morning, I saw a large collection of persons
on the shore nearest the vessel, and many in boats; and was, at
the same time, informed that the moment the troops should be
withdrawn from the brig, an attempt would be made to board
her by force. I was further informed an attempt had already
been made. I have, therefore, to request your excellency will
take such measures as you may deem proper for the protection
of the said vessel and cargo." Bacon was simply trying to conceal his own duplicity.

Sir Francis had probably learned about the Bacon-Gifford
plot, and he responded to Bacon's deceitful letter that same
day: "I beg to state that I cannot think it possible that any of
her Majesty's subjects would act so improperly as to attempt to
board, by force, the American brig *Creole*; and should such an
unauthorized attempt be made, I shall be quite ready to use
every authorized means for preventing it."

The governor must have decided that it was time for the
slaves to be freed. That morning Reverend Poole, chaplain of
the British garrison, and Reverend Aldridge, a clergyman of
one of the Episcopal churches in Nassau, began holding conversations with the slaves, telling them they would soon be liberated. Religious groups were undoubtedly planning to aid the
blacks once they were free.

Meanwhile a flotilla of fifty to sixty "musquito" boats con-
taining black Bahamians was buzzing about the *Creole*. In his
testimony at the insurance trials, Gifford reported his belief
that the civil authorities had hired the "musquito" fleet as part
of the plan to free the slaves. At the same time about fifteen

hundred Bahamians, mostly blacks, were said to be on shore watching the activities around the *Creole*. The Bahamians in boats and on land did not take direct action, and there is no reason to believe that the whites on the *Creole* were in danger. They were, however, undoubtedly intimidated and not likely to try to subdue the Bahamian troops and sail away to New Orleans.

During the morning Bacon was invited to appear before the council, where he learned that the attorney general, the provost marshal, and the police had been ordered to the *Creole* to bring the accused mutineers to shore, in order to avoid any violence from the large number of Bahamians in small boats surrounding the slave ship and from those on shore. The mutineers were to be arrested, but no limits were to be placed on any other slaves who wished to go ashore.

As Attorney General George Anderson approached the *Creole*, he came across the large number of "musquito" boats and urged those on the boats to be peaceful. He was told they were waiting to transport to shore the slaves permitted to quit the *Creole*. Anderson found them without arms, but they did have ten or twelve cudgels, which Anderson threw overboard.

After Anderson boarded the *Creole*, he had the accused mutineers pointed out to him. Before he turned to the British decision about their fate, he addressed all the other slaves from the quarterdeck: "My friends, you have been detained a short time on board of the *Creole*, for the purpose of ascertaining the individuals who were concerned in this mutiny and murder; they have been identified and will be retained; the rest of you are free, and are at liberty to go on shore, and wherever you please."

Anderson then addressed the prisoners: "Men, there are nineteen of you who have been identified as having engaged in the murder of Mr. Hewell, and in an attempt to kill the captain and others; you will be detained and lodged in prison for a time, in order that we may communicate to the English Government, and ascertain whether your trial shall take place here or elsewhere." He gave no indication of another option: free the nineteen without a trial.

This was undoubtedly a bitter moment for Madison Washington and his fellow mutineers. Their actions had freed most of the slaves on the ship, but they faced an uncertain future. We do not know what Madison Washington was saying or thinking during his captivity, for we never hear his voice once he was tied in the longboat. His testimony was apparently not taken by the British, nor do we hear of him from the Nassau prison where he was detained for some five months, until April 1842. It was far from clear what the authorities in London would decide about the fate of Washington and his fellow mutineers.

Attorney General Anderson did offer the mutineers slight hope: he promised to protect their rights. If they wished, they would be given the depositions that included the charges against them and could ask that witnesses be examined to refute those charges. Were these promises kept? Did the nineteen have an attorney? The records are silent. Or were the nineteen secretly told that the officials in London were unlikely to rule against them, that their jailing was a diplomatic ruse? We do not know.

After Anderson had addressed the two groups of blacks, he asked everyone else on the *Creole* to appear on deck. He told Gifford that he intended to remove all restrictions on the free movement of the slaves. According to Anderson, Gifford then said it "was not his desire to detain on board his vessel any one of the persons (shipped as slaves) who did not wish to remain, and that they had his free permission to quit her." Merritt then echoed Gifford's message, saying the slaves "were at perfect liberty to go on shore if they pleased." Both Gifford and Merritt were later to deny making any such statements.

In his testimony at the insurance trials, Gifford gave evidence casting slaves in a bad light the day they were freed. According to his story, before Anderson addressed the slaves, one of the British magistrates told the second mate and some of the seamen to lock up their money and clothes. Merritt reported that his men were frightened and did secure their belongings, but in some cases it was too late: one of the slaves had "put on four pairs of pantaloons another put on two suits."

Later defending himself, Gifford protested that after Anderson told the slaves they were free to go ashore, he objected but Anderson warned him, "You had better not object to it: you had better let them go quietly ashore; if you object, I am afraid there will be blood shed."

After his remarks on the *Creole*, Anderson gave a signal and the "musquito" fleet came alongside the ship. Gifford testified that the magistrates helped the freed slaves into the small boats, and the Americans charged that Anderson, by now in his own boat, went to the individual boats in the "musquito" fleet and shook hands with the newly liberated blacks, congratulating them on their freedom. Gifford may have invented the incident to convince the pro-slavery Americans that the British were too free socially in their relations with blacks. (This incident is also in doubt, however, because Anderson later insisted that the handshakes did not take place.) Gifford and Merritt further contended that Anderson's report of their approval of the freeing of the slaves was untrue.

Bacon was also distressed and wrote to Governor Cockburn on November 14, 1841, protesting the freeing of the slaves and the role of the attorney general during that episode. Bacon had received a report from Gifford, which he obviously believed.

"These slaves," Bacon wrote, "as I view the case, while they were under the American flag, and regularly cleared from one slaveholding State to another, within the United States, were as much a portion of the cargo of the said brig, as the tobacco and other articles on board; and whether on the high seas, or in an English port, does not change their character; and, that her Majesty's Government had not the right to interfere with, or control, the officers of an American vessel, thus circumstanced, in such a course as might be necessary and proper to secure such property from being lost to the owners."

In a letter of great restraint—for Bacon's reference to the slaves as "cargo" must have offended him—Cockburn responded the next day. He was diplomatic, but he agreed with none of Bacon's assertions.

Bacon had been completely foiled by the British officials in Nassau. Cockburn, by his actions, showed that he believed the British policy of emancipating the slaves to be legal and correct. Attorney General Anderson declared that he favored emancipation and that "as slavery is abolished throughout the British dominions, the moment a vessel comes into a British port with slaves on board, to whatever nation such vessel may belong, and however imperious the necessity may have been which drove her into such port, such slaves become immediately entitled to the protection of British laws, and that the right of their owners to treat and deal with them as slaves, ceases."

Anderson insisted that the Nassau Protest contained many fabrications. He asserted that he did not control the "musquito" boats; he did not shake hands with the freed slaves; he did not tell Gifford to make no objection to the slaves' going ashore; he did not say, "You are free and at liberty to go on shore, and wherever you please," for he felt there was no need for authorities to make such a statement.

Each side said to the other, in effect, "You are lying."

After the freed slaves entered Nassau, the Americans on the *Creole* tried to provoke the British officials, refusing their request that the slaves' baggage be turned over to them. Gifford responded that as far as he knew the slaves had no baggage, but if they did it belonged to their owners. The British responded by seizing the baggage and returning it to the freed slaves. Gifford then sought to sell the barrels of salt pork and beef and the hardtack since the slaves were no longer on board to be fed. The British refused to buy the food.

Gifford saw several former *Creole* slaves in Nassau a few days after the liberation. According to his account, they wished to continue on to New Orleans but were afraid of the Bahamians and dared not risk an attempt to board the slave ship. He reported in the New Orleans Protest that a mulatto girl and one called Pinckey wished to be smuggled on board the *Creole*, but he felt it was far too dangerous to do so. Perhaps the slaves Gifford was talking to were playing an elaborate hoax on him. Or perhaps Gifford invented these stories about freed slaves wishing to be reenslaved. Slave owners wanted to believe—against all evidence—that slaves were content with their lot. The *Creole* slaves freed in Nassau could have applied to Bacon for help in being sent on to New Orleans and the slave auction. Bacon would have gone to great lengths to put them back in the hands of slave traders, doing his best to outsmart the British officials. We find no evidence that any freed *Creole* slave in Nassau actually wanted to live and work in sugar and cotton fields in the American South. As far as we can determine, Lewis, McCargo's "faithful" slave, stayed in Nassau.

For reasons that are not entirely clear, five slaves—four women and a child—remained on the *Creole* when the others departed, and these five did go on to New Orleans, continuing in servitude. Two of the women were maids in the cabin—

Rachel Glover, thirty, and a mulatto girl named Mary, who was about thirteen. According to Gifford in his testimony in the insurance trials, on the day of liberation these two were crying and did not know what they should do. It may be that Gifford made them promises about special care and protection if they would go on to New Orleans and become concubines there. Or that the whites on the *Creole* intimidated the black women and forced them to remain on the ship. Two other women who had been kept in the hold also went on to New Orleans. Perhaps the four women were afraid of change, afraid of a new life in a British territory. Rachel's son, who was five, of course followed Rachel's wishes.

Among the main body of *Creole* slaves freed by the British, many were apparently resettled in Jamaica, which was experiencing a depressed economy. A ship with some of the ex-slaves departed from Nassau for Jamaica on November 16, 1841, and another shipload left on December 4. What happened next is not entirely clear. The *Richmond Enquirer* on January 1, 1842, printed a story based on an unsigned letter that originally appeared in the *Charleston Courier* on December 9, 1841, indicating that "a small schooner arrived from Nassau to [Kingston, Jamaica] with about 60 or 70 negroes, and he [the writer of the letter] understands that they were a portion of those taken into Nassau by the brig *Creole*—the inhabitants or authorities would not allow them to land—the schooner was anchored off the town—they were looked upon as a gang of murderers, and the inhabitants did not appear disposed to have any thing to do with them. The schooner was still lying at anchor with the negroes on board when he left."

The information in this letter may be pro-slavery propaganda, or it may be that the schooner was under quarantine for a few days. The citizens of Nassau supported the former slaves and rallied for their freedom. It is difficult to believe that most citizens of Jamaica looked upon these former slaves as "murderers," though plantation owners may have felt otherwise. In the absence of succeeding stories about the schooner in Kingston harbor, we suspect that the freed blacks were eventually allowed to land. If so, did the local government and churches help them? They certainly needed help, just as the runaways who reached Canada needed help.

Other former slaves from the *Creole* may well have remained in the Bahamas, though the economy of those islands was seemingly as depressed as Jamaica's. They arrived penniless, and their baggage, reclaimed from the ship, must have consisted of a few clothes and trinkets and a blanket or quilt.

While Madison Washington and his followers were in jail, two of them died: Adam Carnay from natural causes, and George Grundy from wounds suffered in the affray. The seventeen remaining men were finally released on April 16, 1842, after Sir Francis Cockburn received orders from London. The Law Lords declared that piracy was not involved in the incident, for "the sole object of compelling the *Creole* was to take them to some Port where they might obtain their freedom, and we think that the act of slaves committed with such intent and object does not amount to piracy."

At one point the whites on the *Creole* had had an inkling of the slaves' desires to escape bondage. They noted, after the mutiny was over, that the nineteen had told them, "all they had done was for their freedom." The whites may have been too pro-slavery to understand the meaning of that simple statement.

Cockburn wrote on April 17, 1842, that a special session of the admiralty court had met the day before and found no reason to take action against the remaining mutineers. They were discharged. The chief justice addressed Madison Washington and the sixteen other surviving mutineers: "It has pleased God to set you free from the bonds of slavery; may you hereafter lead the lives of good and faithful subjects of Her Majesty's Government."

Now that the seventeen were free, where would they go? The words of the chief justice probably convinced many of them to remain in a British territory. They certainly knew that the government of the United States would not protect them.

Madison Washington's fate is unknown. In his 1863 essay "Madison Washington," William Wells Brown wrote, "Not many months since, an American ship went ashore at Nassau, and among the first to render assistance to the crew was Madison Washington." Brown omitted that sentence from his 1867 essay "Slave Revolt at Sea," perhaps an indication that the author could not substantiate the story. Did Washington make another trip to Virginia in an attempt to rescue his wife? Or did he remarry? Was his spirit broken by his arrest and imprisonment? Or did his leadership abilities remain intact during the remainder of his life? Did he remain a revolutionary whose later activities are lost to us? And what about Dr. Ruffin, Elijah Morris, Ben Johnstone, and all the other slaves on the *Creole*? The stories of their lives before and after the mutiny are written on water.

. . .*A*fter the mutineers were released from jail, they should have been found and interviewed. Their stories should have been written down. They should have been helped to establish themselves. Madison Washington would have been an excellent lecturer for the abolitionist movement, especially in the British Isles, for he could have spoken eloquently about the effects of the British actions to free the slaves on the *Creole*. He could have described his life in slavery, as Frederick Douglass and many other escaped slaves did. He would have been effective speaking in free states in the United States too, even though the Garrisonians would have objected to him because the mutineers had used violence in their quest for freedom. His impassioned message might have frightened some audiences.

Douglass admired Washington and understood the use of violence on the *Creole*. Douglass made use of Washington in his lectures and in his "The Heroic Slave," but he mythologized the mutineer and seemingly did nothing to help his hero. True, Douglass had no personal resources to find Washington and bring him into the abolitionist cause, but he could have called on his wealthy British and American friends who were in positions to help. He did not do so. Nobody did so, we believe. Madison Washington and his followers were abandoned heroes, but they were free from slavery through their own efforts and with help from British officials. It is our loss that their complete stories have not survived.

VII

The Ensuing Controversies

THE *CREOLE*, now captained by Gifford who was replacing the seriously injured Ensor, sailed from Nassau and arrived in New Orleans on December 2, 1841. News of the mutiny and the British government's freeing of the slaves created a storm. The New Orleans Protest by the white men on the ship—an account biased against the mutineers—was then widely published in newspapers in many parts of the country. Southerners could find in it justification for their repressive measures to maintain control of blacks. Abolitionists had to deconstruct the document in order to justify the mutiny.

Immediately after word of the revolt spread through New Orleans, the *New Orleans Bulletin* on December 16, 1841, announced that the city was "thrown into a flame" and that it was time to settle "whether British authority can strip American citizens of their property without their consent."

The *Charleston Mercury* reported the *Creole* affair as a "new outrage by British colonial authorities on American property." The Southern press was filled with attacks against the British, and many Northern newspapers supported the Southern view. The *New York Herald* noted: "It would be worse than affectation to deny that never since immediately preceding the last war [1812] have relations with England assumed so unpleasant and so gloomy a prospect as they do at the moment."

The pro-slavery faction, in whatever part of the country, was particularly worried because of the *Amistad* decision of the U.S. Supreme Court in March 1841, which had freed Cinqué and the other Africans on that ship. It was feared that property rights were being permanently trampled by the rulings in the *Amistad* and *Creole* cases that freed slaves, effectively confiscating slave owners' "property."

The *Worcester* (Massachusetts) *Spy* did not believe Northerners would go to war with the British "to DEFEND OUR AMERICAN SLAVE TRADE." William Ellery Channing, in a letter to a friend in England, wrote: "The affair has stirred up the South to much angry menace, and one member of Congress has been foolish enough to talk of a retaliatory assault on New Providence. I trust that England will use this opportunity to prove her immovable fidelity to the principles of justice and humanity which she has espoused."

Joshua Giddings, congressman from Ohio, introduced a resolution in the House declaring that the mutineers had "violated no law of the United States" and that efforts to reenslave them were "incompatible with our national honor." When Giddings was then censured by the House by a vote of 125 to 69, he resigned, and was later reelected.

Giddings was a decidedly minority voice in Congress. John C. Calhoun, senator from South Carolina, proposed a *Creole* resolution: President John Tyler was asked to consider official action concerning "the punishment of the guilty, redress of the wrong done to our citizens, and the insult offered to the American flag." Supporting Calhoun's position was Senator William C. Preston, also from South Carolina, who declared that the mutineers "were slaves and not persons."

On January 29, 1842, Secretary of State Daniel Webster expressed the official government position when he directed Edward Everett, U.S. ambassador to Great Britain, to support Calhoun's resolution. The authorities in Nassau, Webster wrote, had a "plain and obvious duty" to aid Bacon and restore the ship and its contents, including the slaves, to the rightful owners. He stated that property should not be "adversely affected by national law" if brought into territorial waters "by force and violence." He believed the slave owners should be indemnified.

In his speech "Slavery, the Slumbering Volcano," delivered in New York on April 23, 1849, Frederick Douglass summarized with irony the British response to the official American position: "The British Government treated it with the utmost deference—for they are a very deferential people. They talked about honorable and right honorable, lords, dukes, and going through all their Parliamentary titles, and sent Lord Ashburton over to this country to tell us of course, that that very deferential people could not send back the 'niggers.' (Laughter and applause.) So Uncle Sam could not get them and he has not got them yet. (Renewed applause.)"

Webster viewed slavery as "a great moral, social, and political evil," but as a constitutionalist he believed that slavery was recognized by the constitution, and he would not interfere with the rights of slaveholders. He also disliked abolitionists, and his political ambitions made possible his easy compromises in support of slavery. His later support of the Fugitive Slave Act of 1850 led John Greenleaf Whittier to write "Ichabod," which begins:

So fallen! so lost! the light withdrawn
Which once he wore!

The glory from his gray hairs gone
  Forevermore!

Revile him not—the Tempter hath
  A snare for all;

And pitying tears, not scorn and wrath,
  Befit his fall!

After verses referring to Webster's "dishonored brow" and suggesting that though his power remained, his honor was dead, the poem concludes,

Then, pay the reverence of old days
  To his dead fame;

Walk backward, with averted gaze,
  And hide the shame!

Long before the Compromise of 1850 with its provisions for the return of fugitive slaves to their owners, Douglass and other leading abolitionists had determined that Webster was not a man of integrity, that he was not to be trusted by those working to end slavery. He was a lost leader.

By the summer of 1842 the *Creole* affair had become an obstacle in settling outstanding boundary and maritime issues between the United States and Great Britain. Lord Ashburton (Alexander Baring of the banking firm) headed a British delegation sent to the United States to resolve the issues. The *Creole* matter was immediately introduced into the discussions, especially the U.S. demand for compensation for the freed slaves. Ashburton had received no instructions for the official British position on that issue. Personally he did not believe that compensation was appropriate.

Abolitionists and foes of slavery were not silent during the tense negotiations. They attacked Webster's positions and actions, arguing that his demands for compensation amounted to approval of the institution of slavery.

Webster negotiated from weakness, for there was no extradition treaty between the two countries that would have forced the British to return the slaves. President Tyler, representing Southern interests, kept inserting himself into the negotiations until the Ashburton mission was in danger of collapse.

Faced with the "great plague" of the *Creole* affair, Ashburton solved the problem by offering vague promises to avoid in the future "officious interference with ships driven by necessity into British ports." Terms such as "officious interference" and "driven by necessity" were not clearly defined. The treaty finally agreed upon called for the extradition of those accused of such crimes as murder or piracy, but these promises were not enforced. Runaway slaves continued to arrive in Canada, and they were not extradited.

The *Creole* rebellion had become a diplomatic matter; its personal issues were largely ignored. Madison Washington and the slaves freed in Nassau were not mentioned by name. Once again, as in the incident in the Bahamas when Governor Cockburn foiled the efforts of Consul Bacon to send all the slaves back to the United States, the British had outwitted American officials.

. . . While newspaper, legislative, and diplomatic discussions about the *Creole* were ongoing, sometimes raging, a legal battle began. McCargo and others who had owned slaves set free in Nassau sued their insurance companies for monetary restitution. The lead attorney for the insurance companies was Judah Philip Benjamin (1811–1884), born to a Sephardic Jewish family in Christiansted, Saint Croix. The Benjamins moved to the

Judah P. Benjamin [Library of Congress]

United States about 1813, first to Wilmington, North Carolina, then to Fayetteville in that state, and finally in 1822 to Charleston, South Carolina. The family arrived in Charleston at the time of the Denmark Vesey slave conspiracy, which culminated in the mass hangings of slaves. Benjamin was then a child, but the events and the public excitement caused by the planned revolt must have influenced his later views about slavery.

Benjamin attended Yale, departing after a scandal of some sort. He then settled in New Orleans, studied law, married into a prominent Creole family, and became a leading attorney and finally United States senator from Louisiana. He was a slave owner and an apologist for the institution. He resigned his Senate seat to join the cabinet of Jefferson Davis and played a prominent role in the Confederacy.

Benjamin's work in the insurance cases was one of his first major successes. His arguments for the insurance companies, first in the lower courts and then in 1845 in the Louisiana Supreme Court, were powerful, controversial, and dramatic. He declared that the *Creole* was not seaworthy "in consequence of not being furnished with arms; from the want of proper precautions and discipline with regard to the slaves; and from the numbers crowded into so small a vessel." He argued "that the whites should have been armed" and "that a strict police should have been maintained. Both were entirely neglected."

Benjamin's contention that the *Creole* was overcrowded certainly appears justified. He carefully noted discrepancies in the accounts of the numbers of slaves on the ship. While the ship officers in the Protests stated that 135 slaves were brought aboard, Benjamin found that 186 was a more likely number. Either number, he insisted, was "excessive cargo" for such a ship of 157 and 25/95 tons. He reckoned that the *Creole* had room for 63 "ordinary passengers" based on the 1819 act of Congress which "forbids the carrying of more than two passengers for every five tons." He noted that the 1819 law was a humane one, for the country wished to encourage immigrants. He then asked, "Will this court be disposed to recognize one standard of humanity for the white man and another for the negro. Will any reasonable man say that 135 negroes would be as cheerful, contented, and indisposed to insurrection, under such circumstances of discomfort, as they would have been in a larger and more commodious vessel?" This argument is similar to Captain Conneau's belief that the rebellion on the *Venus* in 1831 had been caused by the poor conditions that the slaves were forced to endure.

Benjamin contended that the officers and guards on the

Creole were incompetent, that there was no "wholesome discipline" and no "reasonable precautions," especially as the ship approached Bahamian waters. He exaggerated, but not much, when he spoke of "the utter absence of an armament on the part of whites."

Benjamin found it difficult to understand the laxity of the white captain and crew because of the well-known—as he saw it—"nature of the slave, and his ever wakeful and ever active longing after liberty." This recognition that slaves were held against their will shows Benjamin, himself a slave owner, rejecting the views of many Southerners that their slaves were content in bondage.

In one of the insurance trials Benjamin moved into dangerous territory when he spoke with feeling about the nature of the slave: "What is a slave? He is a human being. He has feeling and passions and intellect. His heart, like the white man's, swells with love, burns with jealousy, aches with sorrow, pines under restraint and discomfort, boils with revenge and ever cherishes the desire for liberty. His passions and feelings in some respects may not be as fervid and as delicate as those of the white man, nor his intellect as acute; but passions and feelings he has, and in some respects they are more violent, and consequently more dangerous, from the very circumstances that his mind is comparatively weak, and unenlightened. Considering the character of the slave, and the peculiar passions which, generated by nature, are strengthened and stimulated by his condition, he is prone to revolt in the very nature of things, and ever ready to conquer his liberty where a probable chance presents itself."

Benjamin was a cultured, well-read man, and his words on "What is a slave?" echo certain parts of Shylock's famous lines in *The Merchant of Venice*: "I am a Jew. Hath not a Jew eyes? Hath not a Jew hands, organs, dimensions, senses, affections, passions; fed with the same food, hurt with the same weapons, subject to the same diseases, heal'd by the same means, warm'd and cool'd by the same winter and summer as a Christian is? If you prick us, do we not bleed? If you tickle us, do we not laugh? If you poison us, do we not die? And if you wrong us, shall we not revenge?"

Benjamin had qualified sympathy for the slaves' longing for freedom. Was he influenced by his family history? His Sephardic ancestors had been expelled from Spain by Ferdinand and Isabella and had migrated to Portugal, Holland, England, the British West Indies, and finally to the United States. He was not unaware of anti-Semitism. Or was he being lawyerly, espousing views he did not believe in, as he represented insurance companies that did not wish to pay McCargo and other "owners" for their freed slaves?

The six insurance cases made their way through the lower courts and finally to the Louisiana Supreme Court in March 1845. There Justice Henry Adams Bullard was concerned with this question in coming to his decisions: Was the loss of the slaves caused by mutiny or by the actions of British officials in Nassau? He ruled that the slaves had mutinied, and in six of the eight cases the insurance companies won because the policies did not cover insurrection. Two of the policies did cover mutiny, and therefore the companies were liable in these cases. Eight years later, in 1853, the Anglo-American Claims Commission awarded the United States and the slave owners $110,330 in compensation for the slaves freed by the British. The political and economic wars over the *Creole* mutiny had ended.

Appendices

1. A Fiction: Madison Washington Rewrites Shylock

I was born a slave and called a nigger. A South Carolina senator declared that we slaves were not persons, and it is true we were herded and sold as if we were cattle. I may be black, but I have eyes, organs, bodily proportions, affections, passions. I love the woman I called my wife, but the state did not recognize our union, and none of the people I met on my return trip to Virginia to try to rescue her understood that love. All my slave life I was fed inferior food and lived in a drafty cabin. Cattle on our plantation were better fed than we, and the cattle barns were no worse than our huts. Our children could be sold from us as if they were calves. Our captors knew we bled when they whipped us or when we were bitten by their guard dogs. Our "owners" and overseers could abuse men and women at will, could turn black women into concubines.

I refused to endure slave life and escaped to freedom in Canada, but I left my wife behind, and I knew that I could not be free while she remained a slave. I determined to go back to Virginia and snatch her from her oppressor. I failed. I was captured and sold to a trader. I did not rescue the woman I love. Where she is now I know not, and I think I will never see her again. I was put on the *Creole*, destined for the market in New Orleans and early death in the hot fields. I knew that my life as a slave in Virginia had been degrading, but to be a slave in Louisiana would be intolerable. What could I do? Accept my fate? Pray? Take my life by jumping overboard? Revolt? The decision was easy. Nineteen of us fought for all the slaves on the *Creole* to be free. One brutal guard was killed and the sailors threatened with instant death.

After our mutiny, the government of the United States wanted to reenslave all of us, try some of us as rebels, execute some of us as rebels. That government was always my enemy. The British government freed the slaves after we arrived in Nassau. Although I was jailed for several months, I was eventually released. That government is not my mortal enemy. On my trip from Canada to Virginia, intent as I was on stealing my wife away, I met Quakers who taught peace and compassion, Garrisonians who urged noncooperation with the slave government, and the Reverend Garnet who told me that oppressed people could secure their liberty through resistance. At night, alone in bed, I wonder: "When we revolted, what part should violence and revenge have played? What part mercy?" I keep reaching different conclusions, but I always remember that what we did was for our freedom. My major regret is that my wife is not free, and I must live out my life without her. There are no happy endings in slavery. Only tragedies.

Nassau, New Providence
1 May 1842

2. Madison Washington and Five Writers

The story of Madison Washington and the revolt on the *Creole* was used immediately by abolitionists in newspaper stories for purposes of propaganda. Within a few years after the mutiny, writers began to publish fiction and histories about the incident. In 1853, the same year the British made payment for the *Creole* slaves set free in Nassau, Frederick Douglass published "The Heroic Slave," his account of Madison Washington and the rebellion he led. For his story, Douglass drew from scattered newspaper accounts of the incident, from stories he had heard about Washington told by people who had met the runaway slave, and from several incidents in his own life. Douglass wrote, in effect, a fictionalized slave narrative, a form not new to him since he had already novelized his own autobiography.

Frederick Douglass (1818–1895), fathered by an unknown white man, was born in Maryland to the slave Harriet Bailey and was named Frederick Augustus Washington Bailey. In 1826 he was sent to Baltimore to live with Hugh and Sophia Auld. Sophia taught him to read and write, but her husband made her stop the lessons because learning "would forever unfit him to be a slave." The bright child was forced to continue his education as best he could.

Bailey was returned in 1832 to the Maryland countryside. Less than a docile slave, even under the authority of the brutal slave breaker Edward Covey, Bailey longed for freedom. At the

Covey house on Chesapeake Bay, then filled with sailing ships, Bailey would stand on shore and—as he would later write in his flamboyant style—begin a long soliloquy "with an apostrophe to the moving multitude of ships: You are loosed from your moorings, and are free; I am fast in my chains, and am a slave! You move merrily before the gentle gale, and I sadly before the bloody whip! You are freedom's swift-winged angels, that fly around the world; I am confined in bands of iron. O that I were free!" The previously unmanageable Bailey became temporarily "broken in body, soul, and spirit." When Douglass wrote this soliloquy into Part I of "The Heroic Slave," he wrote admiringly of his hero Washington that, though he has been severely beaten, his spirit has not been broken. He pictures a more heroic Washington than he himself had been in similar circumstances.

After some especially cruel treatment by Covey, Bailey ran away but returned after a short time. Covey tried to tie Bailey up and flog him. Bailey resisted, and upon this unexpected defiance, Covey "trembled like a leaf." Bailey told Covey that he had been "used like a brute for six months" and that he was determined to be so used no longer. The two fought for two hours, and Covey got "the worst end of the bargain." Covey never again laid hands on Bailey. The fight was a turning point in Bailey's life: he regained his self-confidence and his determination to be free.

Bailey's service with Covey was terminated at the end of 1833, and he was then hired out to William Freeland, a comparatively lenient master. It was a relatively happy time for Bailey, who made good friends among the slaves on the farm. Six of them began to plot a way of escaping servitude, but they were betrayed, probably by a black man who was thought to be a friend. Douglass was reticent to make a positive identification of the betrayer. In "The Heroic Slave" the black person who

Frederick Douglass

betrays Washington does so innocently. Douglas seemingly did not wish to admit that blacks sometimes willingly broke faith with other blacks and betrayed them.

Bailey and his fellow conspirators were jailed. A few minutes after they were locked up, slave traders and their agents descended upon the jail to determine if the strong young men were for sale. In his *Narrative of the Life of Frederick Douglass*, he calls these men "fiends from perdition." In the *Narrative* the traders laugh and grin over the slaves, and "one by one went into an examination of us, with intent to ascertain our value." Douglass is more detailed about the examination in *My Bondage*: "Whisky-bloated gamblers" feel their arms and legs and shake the slaves by the shoulders to see if they are healthy.

In those Victorian times Douglass did not write specifically about the sexually charged examinations of disrobed slaves. In "The Heroic Slave" he does not even include a scene at a slave auction or an examination in a jail or slave pen.

After a few days, Bailey's master fetched him from jail and soon sent him back to Baltimore, where he became an apprentice caulker in a shipyard. During his time in Baltimore, he met his future wife, Anna Murray, a free black, and made plans to escape, disguised as a sailor. He began his escape on September 3, 1838, not long before Madison Washington fled Virginia. Douglass was able to reach New York, where he was warned by an acquaintance that some blacks in the city were in the pay of slave owners and would betray him for the bounty. The friend also told him to tell no person that he was a runaway. Bailey was frightened, and in his distress would not at first risk asking directions to the home of David Ruggles (1810–1849), a member of the Vigilance Committee who helped escaped slaves get out of New York to safer communities. Once he met Ruggles, he was protected. In "The Heroic Slave," Douglass gives Washington an abolitionist protector, Mr. Listwell.

Douglass waited in New York for Anna Murray to join him, and as soon as she arrived they were married. Unlike Madison Washington, Douglass was reunited with the woman he loved. The newlyweds left for New Bedford, Massachusetts, where Bailey then assumed the name of Douglass, taken from Sir Walter Scott's *The Lady of the Lake*.

Douglass did manual labor in New Bedford, and not long after he arrived there he began to subscribe to William Lloyd Garrison's abolitionist newspaper, *The Liberator*. Garrison preached noncooperation with what he considered the corrupt national government that recognized slavery. He opposed violence, but his language as speaker and writer was strident. In the first issue of his newspaper, he asserted: "I will not equivo-

William Lloyd Garrison

cate, I will not excuse, I will not retreat a single inch, and I will be heard."

Douglass, who had the rich and powerful voice of a nineteenth-century orator, first spoke at an anti-slavery meeting in 1841, beginning his long career in the movement. He became one of the most influential and best-known opponents of slavery. For several years he was a friend and follower of Garrison. He accepted Garrison's belief that the Constitution was evil because it legalized slavery. Garrison argued that slavery should be resisted with moral persuasion, not violence or political activity.

Soon after Douglass published his *Narrative* in 1845, he went to the British Isles for two years to speak on behalf of the abolition of slavery. British friends purchased his freedom for 150 pounds sterling. By the time of his return to the United States in 1847, Douglass had acquired an international reputation, and he began to distance himself from Garrison. Douglass had been a man of peace, but with the enactment of the Fugitive Slave Law in 1850, he moved inexorably toward the belief that slaves were justified in using violence to gain their freedom. "The Heroic Slave" is one of his most pointed statements on this subject.

In the British Isles and in the United States Douglass often spoke about Madison Washington, presenting an oratorical version of Washington's desire for freedom. He would dramatically recount stories of his hero's escape and recapture, and his role in the *Creole* revolt. Douglass then turned this material into his one and only work of fiction, "The Heroic Slave," which appeared in *Autographs for Freedom* (1853) and in *Frederick Douglass' Paper*.

A handsome man himself, Douglass could not quite make up his mind how to describe Washington's physical appearance. In his powerful lecture "Slavery: The Slumbering Volcano," written not long before "The Heroic Slave," Douglass uses the stereotypical descriptions of a slave to describe Washington: "a black man, with woolly head, high cheek bones, protruding lip, distended nostril, and retreating forehead." It was just such a person, without embellished characteristics, Douglass proclaimed, who could liberate a slave ship.

In "The Heroic Slave," Douglass offers an idealized portrait of Washington, incorporating many of his own physical characteristics into his rather overheated descriptive language: "Madison was of manly form. Tall, symmetrical, round, and strong. In his movements he seemed to combine, with the strength of the lion, a lion's elasticity. His torn sleeves disclosed arms like polished iron. His face was 'black, but comely.' His eye, lit with emotion, kept guard under a brow as dark and as glossy as the raven's wing. His whole appearance betokened Herculean strength; yet there was nothing savage or forbidding in his aspect. A child might play in his arms, or dance on his shoulders. A giant's strength, but not a giant's heart was in him. His broad mouth and nose spoke only of good nature and kindness. But his voice, that unfailing index of the soul, though full and melodious, had that in it which could terrify as well as charm. He was just the man you would choose when hardships were to be endured, or danger to be encountered—intelligent and brave. He had a head to conceive, and the hand to execute. In a word, he was one to be sought as a friend, but to be dreaded as an enemy."

Douglass was making this revolutionary leader acceptable to a white audience. His newspaper had a great many white readers, and he knew that a huge black man (even if fictional), without redeeming qualities of goodness and kindness, was likely to be considered threatening and dangerous.

"The Heroic Slave," written in four parts, begins with a meditation on Virginia as the home of statesmen and heroes, especially Patrick Henry, Thomas Jefferson, and George Washington. The unnamed narrator declares that he will write about a man who loved liberty as fervently as any of these three notables, about an undeservedly obscure person who fought for freedom against great odds.

After this prologue in Part I, the novella begins in the spring of 1835 as a Northern man, riding through Virginia, stops to allow his horse to drink. From the pine forest the man hears a voice of someone beset by woe. In the soliloquy that follows, the speaker reveals himself as a much abused and mistreated slave: "I am no coward. Liberty I will have, or die in the attempt to gain it." The traveler, identified as a Mr. Listwell, listens to the story, which is very similar to Douglass's soliloquy on Chesapeake Bay. Listwell, appropriately named, does manage a glimpse of the manly Madison but is not himself seen. The lament he has heard is so powerful that Listwell is instantly converted to abolitionism—certainly one of the major aims of the slave narrative.

In Part II, set in the winter of 1840, the reader is taken into the Ohio farm home of the Listwells. It is to be a night of coincidences and hard-to-believe events. Monte, the Listwells' dog, hears something, growls, barks, and then stops, for he senses the presence of a friend. A tall man appears at the door, and Listwell recognizes him as the slave he had heard and seen in Virginia. The black man then introduces himself as Madison Washington, now an escaped slave on his way to freedom in Canada. Washington tells his story, beginning with an account of why he was in distress that day in the Virginia forest. Douglass was here writing from his own knowledge of the mistreatment of slaves.

Madison tells of a whipping he received after he had overstayed a visit to a mill. The delay was not his fault, he told his master and the overseer, but they allowed no excuses.

"Hold your tongue, you impudent rascal," was the response to each of Washington's explanations. The slave was then tied to a tree; his feet were chained together, and a heavy bar was placed between his ankles before he was given forty lashes. The overseer then poured brine over Washington's bleeding back to cause him more pain and to prevent infections. Washington vowed to run away and did so when his master had gone to church on Sunday. Douglass expected his readers to feel revulsion at the hypocrisy of the religious master and at the pro-slavery ministers throughout the South who defended the system.

Washington's flight, according to the story, was initially aborted. He lost his way, traveled in a circle, and came back to his original starting point. He spoke with his wife and then hid out in the nearby woods and swamp. (Hiding out was common throughout the slaveholding states.) Washington stayed in the forest for five years, with weekly night visits from his wife. Douglass gives the name Susan to Madison's wife, information missing from the *Friend of Man* article. Did Douglass learn her name from those who met the runaway on his trip back to Virginia, or did Douglass simply invent the name? He gives no description of Susan. Was she plain, as Douglass's own first wife was? Or was she beautiful? We do not know.

Douglass in his writings was consistently restrained in his comments about women and about sexual matters. His own marriage to Anna Murray was often not a happy one, in part because she was illiterate and did not share his intellectual interests. In the fictional story Douglass gives Madison and Susan a sexual life, for they are said to have two small children. In the later sections of the story the children are not mentioned, a curious lapse on the part of the author.

Washington eventually fled the dismal swamp where he had lived for years only because of a raging fire that forced him from his hiding place. Here Douglass calls upon his knowledge that many runaways did not run far, but the length of time he places Madison in the swamp is unusual. Douglass knew Harriet A. Jacobs and her brother John S. Jacobs and was perhaps drawing on their stories of Harriet's hiding in an attic for almost seven years.

Douglass has Madison explain to the Listwells, who give him a good meal that night, his justification for stealing food during his journey northward: "Your moral code may differ from mine. . . . The fact is, sir, during my flight I felt myself robbed by society of all my just rights; that I was in an enemy's land, who sought both my life and my liberty. They had transformed me into a brute; made merchandise of my body, and for all the purposes of my flight, turned day into night,—and guided by my own necessities, and in contempt of their conventionalities, I did not scruple to take bread where I could get it." Douglass knew from experience that escaping slaves had to lie and steal if they wished to survive. Douglass also used this episode to make a bow to the wealthy Gerrit Smith, a rival of Garrison's. Listwell tells Madison that he had once had doubts about that point of view, but Smith convinced him of the reasonableness of such action. Smith did make generous contributions to Douglass's publications and was praised for his support of many black causes.

During his talk with the Listwells, Washington tells of a betrayal while on his journey toward Canada. He had given a dollar to an old black man to buy supplies for him. At the store the old man was accused of stealing the money. He was whipped, and the "truthfulness" of his character made him reveal that a runaway had given him the money. Fourteen men with guns scoured the woods for Washington but failed to find him. Washington defends the old man, asserting that he was not to blame. Again, Douglass was fictionalizing his own betrayal at the time of his escape attempt.

Listwell helps Madison escape to Canada. Washington then writes to declare that he has arrived safely. Douglass assumes, without evidence, as far as we can determine, that Washington could read and write at the time he arrived in Canada. Again, Douglass seems to be writing about himself in this story, for he was literate before he escaped from Maryland. Washington writes this letter to the Listwells: "Madison is out of the woods at last; I nestle in the mane of the British lion, protected by his mighty paw from the talons and the beak of the American eagle. I AM FREE, and breathe an atmosphere too pure for *slaves*, slave-hunters, or slave holders. My heart is full. As many thanks to you, sir, and to your kind lady, as there are pebbles on the shores of Lake Erie; and may the blessings of God rest upon you both. You will never be forgotten by your profoundly greatful friend." These words are vintage Douglass, completely different from the plain-spoken Madison Washington whose voice is heard in Senate Documents, No. 51, the official account of the *Creole* mutiny (see the Note on Sources).

In Part III the scene shifts to a derelict inn about fifteen miles from Richmond, Virginia. The building and grounds are in disrepair, indicating how Southern society has been corrupted by slavery. Listwell is again in Virginia, but why he is there is never explained. By happenstance, Madison Washington appears, in a coffle on his way to Richmond, where he is to be sent to the slave market in New Orleans.

Madison explains to Listwell that the desire to free his wife—the children are not mentioned—brought him back to Virginia. He hid in the old neighborhood for a week waiting for his chance to spirit Susan away. He used a ladder to reach her room, but Susan was frightened when he raised the window. She screamed and then fainted. He began to carry her down the ladder, but the dogs and the white people in the house were aroused. The cool air revived Susan, and she recognized her husband. The two fled, followed by the vicious dogs and Washington's old master and his two sons.

"*Stop! Stop! or be shot down,*" was shouted, but the couple did not stop. Shots rang out; Susan was killed, and Washington was wounded and overpowered. Douglass, with his tragic view of slavery, would not allow Susan to survive. He knew there was little chance for a happy ending for slaves such as Madison or Susan.

Douglass then envisioned that the wounded Washington would have been chained for three days, during which time he was put on public display: "All the slaves, for miles around, were brought to see me. Many slaveholders came with their slaves, using me as proof of the completeness of their power, and of the impossibility of slaves getting away. I was taunted,

133

jeered at, and berated by them, in a manner that pierced me to the soul. Thank God, I was able to smother my rage, and to bear it all with seeming composure." After his wounds are almost healed, he is stripped, tied to a tree, and given sixty lashes. Soon afterward he is sold to a slave trader.

In Douglass's narrative, when Mr. Listwell comes upon Washington in the coffle and hears his story of recapture and sale, he inquires: "Do you think your master would sell you to me?"

The slave responds: "O no, sir! I was sold on condition of my being taken South. The motive is revenge."

Listwell's response is one acceptable to Stowe's Uncle Tom: "I fear I can do nothing for you. Put your trust in God, and bear your sad lot with the manly fortitude which becomes a man. I shall see you at Richmond, but don't recognize me."

"With a sad heart," Listwell follows the coffle to Richmond. Douglass tells his readers that the slave drivers lashed the slaves who faltered. As Listwell makes his way to the wharf, Douglass has him reject his earlier belief that he can do nothing to help Washington: "The thought struck him that, while mixing with the multitude, he might do his friend Madison one last service, and he stepped into a hardware store and purchased three strong *files*. These he took with him and standing near the small boat, which lay in wait to bear the company by parcels to the side of the brig that lay in the stream, he managed, as Madison passed him, to slip the files into his pocket, and at once darted back among the crowd."

Listwell thus plays a major role in the mutiny, providing the means for the slaves to rid themselves of their hated chains. Douglass seems reluctant in this scene to allow Washington the determined power and initiative to provide his own files. Douglass may well have known that files were not necessary, for the slaves on the *Creole* were not chained. But his account of Washington and his followers freeing themselves from their restraints makes a good story.

Part IV of "The Heroic Slave" is set in a coffee house in Richmond, two months after the mutiny has taken place. The speakers are Jack Williams, a sailor who was not on the ship but has heard about the affray, and Grant, the first mate on the slave ship. Williams argues, "Those black rascals got the upper hand of ye altogether; and, in my opinion, the whole disaster was the result of ignorance of the real character of *darkies* in general. With half a dozen *resolute* white men . . . I could have had the rascals in irons in ten minutes. . . ."

Grant, loosely modeled on First Mate Gifford, argues, "It is quite easy to talk of flogging niggers here on land, where you have the sympathy of the community, and the whole physical force of the government, State and national. . . . I deny that the negro is, naturally, a coward, or that your theory of managing slaves will stand the test of salt water."

Rather than deal directly with the mutiny, Douglass made a strategic decision to have Grant describe what happened on the *Creole*. While Washington is allowed to speak, the events are not seen from his point of view.

Grant reports that Washington had files with him and managed to get the irons off himself and eighteen others. The attack began at twilight, just after Grant had seen Washington at a hatchway looking "good-natured." The captain and Jameson, said to be the owner of most of the slaves and a fictional version of Hewell, were on deck and armed. Suddenly there was a shot, and nineteen unfettered slaves rushed the deck. Grant tried to draw his knife but was knocked out. When he awoke, the captain and Jameson were dying. Douglass does not confront the issue of which slaves were responsible for the killings.

Grant also found that the sailors were in the rigging. He tried to get them to come down and retake the ship, but they stayed where they were. He then advanced on Washington, who told him, "Sir, your life is in my hands. I could have killed you a dozen times over during the last half hour, and could kill you now. You call me a black murderer. I am not a murderer. God is my witness that LIBERTY, not malice, is the motive for this night's work."

In Douglass's version, a storm strikes, and the bodies of the captain and Jameson are swept overboard. Douglass undoubtedly knew that the slaves mutilated the body of Hewell and then tossed it overboard, but he softens the scene by having high waves claim the bodies of the two slain white men.

In Grant's account, Washington becomes the captain of the ship and is at the helm. This is fiction, but it is true that Washington was in charge after the revolt. Douglass does, however, reflect the justified fear of the slaves that Grant, supposedly helping to steer the ship into a British-controlled port, is not to be trusted and will try to land in a slave port.

In Douglass's story, Grant admits that he felt Madison Washington to be a superior person, something that Gifford on the *Creole* did not do. Grant speaks of the "dignity of his manner and the eloquence of his speech. It seemed as if the souls of both the great dead (whose names he bore) had entered him." Douglass is certainly writing himself into the story here, for he was an eloquent speaker, and Washington was part of his birth name.

Douglass concludes with Grant telling what happened when the *Creole* reached Nassau. Black soldiers came on board, and these "impudent rascals" did not recognize "persons as property." The slaves left the ship "amidst the deafening cheers of a multitude of sympathizing spectators, under the triumphant leadership of their heroic chief and deliverer MADISON WASHINGTON." This ending is certainly fiction, for Washington and his followers left the ship for jail. The actions of Governor

Cockburn and other British officials are largely ignored, as is the perfidy of the United States consul.

"The Heroic Slave" contains too many unbelievable coincidences, and Douglass's overblown language seems out of keeping with the subject matter. His story would have been more successful had he used Washington as a first-person narrator, but he may have decided against that strategy because Washington as narrator of the mutiny might well have frightened many white readers.

Washington and his followers did defeat the slave owners, the slave dealers, the slave transporters, and the slave-supporting U.S. government. Douglass makes these points and is particularly convincing in portraying the cruelties Washington would have suffered in slavery and his heroic qualities.

. . . *W*illiam Wells Brown (1814?–1884) also wrote about Madison Washington and the *Creole*. Brown was born near Lexington, Kentucky, to a white man and a slave. He spent his early working years in St. Louis, hired out to James Walker, a slave trader, with whom he made three trips to the slave market in New Orleans. In his *Narrative of William W. Brown, A Fugitive Slave* he describes some of his duties. Walker took several weeks to purchase the slaves to go on the auction block, and they were taken by steamboat to New Orleans. Walker was an unscrupulous businessman: Brown was told to prepare the older men for sale; grey whiskers were pulled from their face, or if there were too many of them the beard was colored with blacking.

On one trip Walker singled out for special attention the beautiful quadroon Cynthia. He had Brown place her in a special stateroom. Brown listened at the door to hear Walker's "vile proposals"—Walker wanted to make Cynthia his mistress and establish her on his farm. If she did not agree, he would sell her as a field hand. Cynthia rejected the offer that night, and Walker left the room.

The next morning Cynthia told her story to Brown "and bewailed her sad fate with floods of tears. I comforted and encouraged her all I could, but I foresaw but too well what the result must be." Brown is silent about what happened to Cynthia on the trip down river, but he does write that Cynthia gave in to Walker's demands and had four of his children before he married and sold her and the children into what Brown calls "hopeless bondage."

Brown offers graphic details of the cruelties suffered by slaves. Not surprisingly, he himself was determined to run away. His first attempt failed, but he succeeded in 1834, when he was aided by Mr. and Mrs. Wells Brown, a Quaker family, whose name he took in appreciation of their kindness.

Brown's autobiography was well received, and in 1853 he published the first novel written by an African American. *Clotel: Or, the President's Daughter* was printed in England for the abolitionist audience there. The novel makes it clear that Brown's ideal black woman was actually an octoroon with many Anglo-Saxon features. Brown describes Clotel: She is as white as any of the traders, "her features as finely defined as any of her sex of pure Anglo Saxon." She is "tall and graceful." Brown makes specific fictional use of the widespread stories that Thomas Jefferson had fathered several children with his slave Sally Hemings.

Brown considered himself an historian of the black experience in the United States, and he wrote about many notable blacks. He first turned his attention to Madison Washington in 1863, in *The Black Man, His Antecedents, His Genius, and His Achievements.* In 1880 he included his Washington chapter in *The Negro in the American Rebellion, His Heroism and His Fidelity,* making only minor changes. While his intentions are

William Wells Brown

laudable, his history of Madison Washington is flawed. Brown seems to have made use of Douglass's "The Heroic Slave," the *Friend of Man* short article on Washington, and other newspaper pieces at the time of the *Creole* revolt. But his history of Washington is based largely on suppositions about the revolutionary leader and his wife.

While Brown made use of Douglass's story, he apparently recognized that the Listwell scenes in "The Heroic Slave" were fiction, and he dropped them. He invents a Canadian farmer who employs Madison. Brown has Madison tell this Mr. Dickson that he has been held by three different men, but he has refused to call them master. Brown also uses the exaggerated language of Douglass: "The birds in the trees and the wild beasts of the forest made me feel that I, like them, ought to be free."

In Brown's account, when Washington is twenty he falls in love with Susan, the beautiful octoroon descended from a participant in the Revolutionary War who had served in both Houses of Congress. She is described in much the same way Brown pictured Clotel as Jefferson's daughter.

Madison plans to escape with Susan before their marriage, but instead they marry first. When their plans are discovered, Washington flees into the forest, but only for months. Brown explains that Washington remained for a time in Virginia hoping to organize an insurrection of local slaves. Brown apparently expected his readers to make connections with Nat Turner's organization of slaves. Without any historical evidence, Brown apparently wants to make Washington into an activist even before he leads a revolt. When Washington's plans fail, he flees to Canada.

Brown has Washington tell farmer Dickson that it will take him five years to make enough money to purchase his wife, and in the meantime she may be sold away. He is determined to return to Virginia to liberate her. Dickson tries to dissuade Washington, but without success. The runaway procures files and saws and hides them in the lining of his coat—unlike Douglass's account in which Listwell provides these instruments so that Madison escapes with white help.

Washington returns to Virginia, and Brown follows Douglass in describing the recapture of the escaped slave. Washington goes to his wife's room too early and is seen by the overseer, who calls to other white men for help. Madison fights valiantly and "laid three of his assailants upon the ground with his manly blows. . . ." But he is injured, weakened by loss of blood, and captured. Susan, however, is not killed, as she is in "The

Heroic Slave," and Brown sets the stage for a melodramatic happy ending.

Now Brown shifts his story to the *Creole*. Following New Orleans newspaper reports of the revolt, Brown misspells the captain's name as Enson, and he asserts, as Douglass did, that the male slaves were "kept in chains while on the voyage." The government document and the records of the insurance trials show this to be untrue. Brown emphasizes Washington's role in planning the mutiny. Like Douglass, he does not give credit to Elijah Morris, Ben Johnstone, Dr. Ruffin, and others for their efforts in carrying out the revolt.

On the ninth day of the voyage, Brown writes, there is a storm at sea and many slaves are ill. In fact a strong breeze came up during the mutiny, but Brown realized that a storm would add drama to the story. Because of the weather, the guards are not watchful, and the nineteen male slaves, freed from their shackles by Washington's files, reach the quarterdeck where the captain and Merritt are standing and where Hewell is sitting on the covering of the head of a companionway, smoking a cigar. Most of the crew are also on deck. Hewell draws his horse pistol and kills one of the slaves. (Brown wants to make the whites responsible for the first killing.) Washington, using a capstan bar, kills Hewell—another ahistorical event, for it was Johnstone and Morris who stabbed Hewell to death. According to Brown, the first and second mates are disabled, and the sailors climb the rigging. Washington, now in control, orders the sailors down and dresses their wounds himself. He orders no more shedding of blood.

The next morning Captain Washington orders a special breakfast for all the slaves. In a melodramatic scene the beautiful Susan appears. Brown describes her: "Though not tall, she yet had a majestic figure. Her well-molded shoulders, prominent bust, black hair which hung in ringlets, mild blue eyes, finely-chiseled mouth, with a splendid set of teeth, a turned and well-rounded chin, skin marbled with the animation of life, and veined by blood given to her by her master, she stood as the representative of two races." Washington, according to Brown, was pure African. Brown's ideal male is purely black and without white blood, but his ideal female is mostly white.

The *Friend of Man* article had raised the possibility that Susan might have been on the *Creole*. Brown, in his history of Washington and the mutiny, makes the speculations come true: Susan is on the ship and is reunited with her husband, a scene as unconvincing as Jim's sudden emancipation at the end of the *Adventures of Huckleberry Finn*. There is no evidence that Susan was on the *Creole*.

In Brown's version, once the ship reaches Nassau the slaves are immediately freed, something we know to be untrue. The slaves, Brown insists, are greeted and protected by the local inhabitants. True, but he ignores the actions of the British officials in arranging to set the slaves free, and ignores the imprisonment and final release of the mutineers. Brown notes that Daniel Webster demanded the return of the slaves but that the British would not agree. Brown then makes an important point in somewhat clearer fashion than Douglass had done in his story: "Had the '*Creole*' revolters been white, and committed their noble act of heroism in another land, the people of the United States would have been the first to recognize their claims."

As an historian, Brown was less than accurate in his use of known information about Madison Washington. Brown's account is flamboyantly written and is more fiction than fact, but his essays on Madison Washington did keep the story alive.

... *T*he third writer to take up the Madison Washington story was Lydia Maria Child (1802–1880), the Massachusetts-born white abolitionist. In 1821 she went to live with her brother, a Harvard graduate who was minister of a Unitarian church in Watertown, Massachusetts. There she came into contact with transcendentalists and abolitionist activists. While teaching in a school for girls, she published two novels, *Hobomok* and *The Rebels*, reflecting her evolving views on social matters.

In 1826 she began a successful magazine for children, *Juvenile Miscellany*. Two years later she married David Child, an abolitionist, and her views grew more radical and more concerned with social reform.

In 1841 she became editor of the *National Anti-Slavery Standard* published in New York. She was a Garrisonian, believing in nonviolence and noncooperation with the federal government. Because she refused to support violent activities to end slavery, she was forced out of that editorship after two years. She did, however, continue to support various abolitionist causes. In 1861 she edited Harriet A. Jacobs's *Incidents in the Life of a Slave Girl*, and in 1865 she prepared a reader called *The Freedmen's Book* for newly freed blacks. This anthology contained a chapter on Madison Washington and the *Creole* episode. Child made her intentions clear in the opening sentence of the work: "I have prepared this book expressly for you, with the hope that those of you who can read will read it aloud to others, and that all of you will derive strength and courage from this true record of what colored men have accomplished, under great disadvantages."

Child's aim was laudable, but her account of Madison Washington, presented as truth, is largely fiction. For her essay on Madison Washington and his wife Susan, she adapted William

Wells Brown's account, toning down several of his more bombastic statements. Brown's chapter on Madison Washington seems to be her only source.

Child refrains from describing Washington as "large and strong," for that might have made him appear dangerous and menacing. And as a Garrisonian she does not wish to appear to condone violence. She does say that "Nature had in fact made him too intelligent and energetic to be contented in Slavery." In addition, he has a "manly air," and "he looked like a being that would never consent to wear a chain." Child presents him as an African—an "unmixed black." Susan, however, is described as an octoroon, fathered by her master. Child omits Brown's statement that Susan was a descendant of a Revolutionary War hero. In Child's account, Susan has blue eyes and glossy dark hair, generally following Brown's description of her, though Child does not mention Susan's "prominent bosom" as Brown had. Child's major contribution to the story of Susan is to suggest the sexual fate of a beautiful black woman: "a handsome woman, who is a slave, is constantly liable to insult and wrong."

At the end of the story, as Susan and Madison are reunited, Child envisions their life together in a British colony "where the laws would protect their domestic happiness." Child apparently made no effort to discover the truth as she imposed a happy conclusion to the tragic love story of the Washingtons.

Child's reconstruction of the life of Madison and Susan and the account of the revolt are primarily the stuff of fiction, cribbed shamelessly from Brown's supposedly true story. The emancipated slaves for whom she wrote this story would have understood a less romanticized version, for their own lives had been difficult and had few happy endings. To read about a heroic Madison who helped free a boatload of slaves would have given them pleasure, but they would also have understood Madison's distress, anger, and guilt because he would never again see his wife, who was either dead or remained in captivity.

... *T*he last of Douglass's contemporaries to write about Madison Washington and the *Creole* affair was Pauline Elizabeth Hopkins (1859–1930). She was a descendant of the black poet and activist James Whitfield, and grew up in Boston, a member of a black family with many abolitionist ties. Graduating from Girls High School, she early began a career as writer, actress, and singer. Her first play, written when she was twenty, was *Slaves' Escape; or The Underground Railroad*, performed by the Hopkins Colored Troubadors, with Hopkins taking the lead role.

In 1900 she began to publish in the *Colored American Magazine*, established in Boston, a magazine to provide for "the flowering of any black talent that had been suppressed by a lack of encouragement and opportunity to be published." She published short stories, nonfiction, and three novels in the periodical, including her fictionalized account of the *Creole* episode titled "A Dash for Liberty" (August 1901).

In many of her writings Hopkins presented African Americans who were models for their race. When she wrote about Washington and his wife, she turned to Brown's account for many specific details. She did, however, make a major change in the name of the hero: she substituted "Monroe" for "Washington," perhaps because she opposed the accommodationist ideas of Booker T. Washington. In doing so, Hopkins signaled that she was fictionalizing the story of Madison Washington.

Hopkins followed Brown, who followed Douglass, in describing Washington as "an unmixed African," handsome and well built. She looked to Brown for information and had Susan's white grandfather serving in the Revolutionary War and in both houses of Congress. Susan is described as a beautiful octoroon with a "superb figure," though Hopkins omits Brown's reference to Susan's "prominent bust."

Douglass, Brown, Child, and Hopkins all asserted that Washington was of pure African blood, noble, a leader of men. They do not seem to be able to imagine that in his years of servitude his body had been marked by the whip or that he was emaciated because of the poor diet afforded slaves. All the writers except Douglass imagine Susan to be beautiful and almost white. Douglass did not describe her. Child believed that a beautiful female slave was certainly vulnerable to the sexual desires of white men, and Hopkins later developed this idea. Brown, Child, and Hopkins were unable to believe that Susan could have been "pure African," as Washington was said to be. Readers may envision her as black and beautiful. Why not think of Washington as having had a white father, as Douglass and Brown had?

Hopkins divides her story into four parts. The first, set in Canada, has Washington explaining to Mr. Dickson why he is intent upon returning to Virginia. It contains some dialogue not in Brown, but the basic details are from Brown.

The second part is set in Virginia and tells the story of Washington's attempt to rescue his wife. Again, the overall details are from Brown, but Hopkins adds local color. The slaves at a cornhusking sing a song beginning

All dem purty gals will be dar,
    Shuck dat corn before you eat.

The slaves (except for Madison) speak in a vaguely comic dialect. In Senate Documents, No. 51, and in the *Creole* accounts by Douglass, Brown, and Child, the slaves speak standard English. In Senate Documents, No. 51, though, slaves do curse. It is reasonable to speculate that the historical Washington spoke in Virginia slave dialect, lightly changed by his short stay in Canada.

Hopkins invents details about Washington's capture. Judge Johnson, Susan's owner and presumably Washington's too, did not want him killed because he was valuable: "Five hundred dollars for him alive!"

In part three, set on the *Creole*, Susan is described by the overseer as a fine "piece of flesh," certain to sell for a high price in New Orleans. The captain, not given a name, admires her beauty and assigns her to a private stateroom. Hopkins obviously had read Brown's autobiography and was drawing on his story of Cynthia.

Hopkins follows Brown in omitting the fictional Listwell, and in her account, as in Brown, the revolting slaves do not receive help from a white man. Washington brings aboard the ship files and saws that he has himself procured. Chained, he does not know that Susan is on the *Creole*.

Writing for a black readership, Hopkins dramatizes the vulnerability of black women in a slave society. She writes melodramatically: "The octoroon lay upon the floor of her cabin, apparently sleeping, when a shadow darkened the door, and the captain stepped into the room, casting bold glances at the reclining figure."

The captain kisses Susan on the lips, and she awakes with a start and begins hitting his face. Hopkins wants her readers to know that Susan will not willingly accept advances from a white man. The captain, a traditional villain, then says, "None of that, my beauty. . . . Why did you think you had a private cabin, and all the delicacies of the season? Not to behave like a young catamount, I warrant you." Hopkins sets the scene for a rape, but she allows Susan to escape.

Susan strikes the captain across the eyes and runs from the stateroom, apparently planning to go overboard. "God have mercy!" she cries as she passes the men's cabin. Washington, who does not recognize her voice, calls out to the damsel in distress, "Hold on, girl; we'll protect you." He breaks his chains, and the flying padlock hits the captain, rendering him unconscious. Madison then calls on his eighteen followers, who have filed through their chains, to begin their revolt.

The ship is soon taken by the slaves, with only two deaths. Hopkins follows Brown in her account of this episode. Washington remains unaware that the "girl" he rushes to protect is his wife. The next morning Susan comes to breakfast:

"Madison!"

"My God! Susan! My wife!"

"She was locked to his breast; she clung to him convulsively. Unnerved at last by the revulsion to more than relief and ecstasy, she broke into wild sobs, while the astonished company closed around them with loud hurrahs."

Hopkins's story is seriously flawed, but she does clearly render Susan's vulnerability to sexual abuse. Writing for a black audience allowed Hopkins more freedom, but Victorian rectitude restrained her from writing even more realistically about Susan as a sexual object.

. . . *T*he most recent literary artist to dramatize the *Creole* affair is Theodore (Ted) Ward (1902–1983), called the "dean of black dramatists." Ward was born in Thibodeaux, Louisiana, and attended school through the seventh grade. After his mother died when he was thirteen, he left home for several years of wandering, during which time he worked as bootblack, barbershop porter, bellhop, and other odd jobs. From his winnings of $2,800 in a gambling house in Chicago he was able to take extension courses at the University of Utah. He then received a scholarship to the University of Wisconsin, where from

Theodore (Ted) Ward [courtesy Laura Branca]

1931 to 1933 he studied creative writing. He worked on a one-act play, *Sick and Tiahd,* later called *Sick and Tired,* completed in 1934. That play, produced in Chicago in 1937, is set in the Mississippi Delta and deals with the life of a black sharecropper. The next year the Chicago Federal Theatre, Negro Unit, produced Ward's first full-length play, *Big White Fog: A Negro Tragedy.* The play explores the radical ideas of the black activist Marcus Garvey and of communism as choices for blacks in the racist society of the United States.

From Chicago, Ward moved to New York where he joined with Langston Hughes and Richard Wright in founding the Negro Playwrights Company. Their first production in 1940, in a Harlem theatre, was *Big White Fog*. The leftist elements of the play were attacked in the press, and in an interview Ward charged that the "vicious reviews" of the drama critics "literally destroyed" the company. He began to have difficulty getting his plays produced, and most of his vast output remains unknown. He did, though, receive many prestigious awards and grants, among them a Guggenheim to work on a play about John Brown, the white abolitionist. *John Brown* was produced in New York in 1950.

In the 1960s Ward was again in Chicago heading the South Side Center of the Performing Arts. He was dedicated to producing plays by black dramatists, but his own dramas were thought to be too radical for audiences then. He was a pioneer in black drama and is certainly an undeservedly neglected playwright.

Ward's *Madison*, suggested by Douglass's "The Heroic Slave," has never been produced or printed. He conceived of the work as a folk opera or folk musical with a realistic setting and characters but with some of the artificiality of the musical form. The set is a cross section of the *Creole*, with action taking place on the quarterdeck and in the lower slave hold. A black half-curtain is used to divide the two parts of the set. The hold is hot, fetid, and crowded, and even when the action is on the quarterdeck and the half-curtain is over the hold, cries and moans can be heard from the slaves in their quarters. The tragic situation of humans being transported for sale at auction is present from the first scene.

In the drama the strong, often silent Washington grieves over the death of his wife. He is presented not as a stand-alone hero but as one who takes collective action for the good of all the slaves on the ship. Ward must have had in mind casting that role with a powerful actor-singer similar to Paul Robeson, who shared many of Ward's social and political beliefs.

Ward introduces a significant number of slaves on the ship, including a group from the same Virginia plantation who were being sold because their owner had been poisoned by the slave woman Zora, who is shunned by many of the other slaves. The owner had wanted Zora to mate with the despicable Big Turp, and to foil that plan she fed her owner poisoned mushrooms. Among the slaves are two young lovers who provide comic relief.

Ward introduces a religious slave, Deacon Albery, who argues as Uncle Tom did, that masters should be obeyed. Washington's vehement rejoinder—that defiance and rebellion are necessary to fight enslavement—is powerfully presented. The philosophical and physical conflicts of Albery and his followers versus Washington and his followers are successfully dramatized.

Douglass, Brown, Child, and Hopkins were hesitant about introducing a full account of the battle between the slaves and the whites on the *Creole*, but Ward was willing to present more scenes from the mutiny itself on stage. Ward's libretto contains many moving and powerful scenes. Had he been able to get *Madison* produced, he undoubtedly would have made needed changes in language and in tempo during the rehearsals. Even with its weaknesses, *Madison* (1956) is the most compelling of all the literary and historical presentations about Washington and the mutiny on the *Creole*. It deserves to be printed and staged.

Madison Washington's love for his wife posed special problems for William Wells Brown, Lydia Maria Child, and Pauline Elizabeth Hopkins, for they wanted a happy ending to the story. Their accounts were ahistorical and melodramatic, with Madison and Susan reunited after the mutiny had taken place. Frederick Douglass and Theodore Ward have Susan killed during Washington's attempt to rescue her. Their tragic view may also ignore historical evidence, for there is no record of Susan's fate. All five writers did understand, though, the importance of the slaves' struggle for liberty, and all emphasized the heroic qualities of Madison Washington.

Bibliography

Ammons, Elizabeth, ed. *Short Fiction by Black Women, 1900–1920.* New York: Oxford University Press, 1991.

Andrews, William L. "The Novelization of Voice in Early African American Autobiography." *PMLA* 105 (January 1990): 23–34.

Bartlett, Irving H. *Daniel Webster.* New York: W. W. Norton, 1978.

Baym, Nina, general ed. *The Norton Anthology of American Literature.* New York: W. W. Norton, 1998.

Blassingame, John W. *The Slave Community: Plantation Life in the Antebellum South,* revised and enlarged edition. New York: Oxford University Press, 1979.

Brown, John. *Slave Life in Georgia.* Savannah: Beehive Press, 1991.

Brown, William Wells. *Clotel, or The President's Daughter* (1853) in *Three Classic African-American Novels,* ed. by Henry Louis Gates, Jr. New York: Vintage Books, 1990.

———. *Narrative of William W. Brown, A Fugitive Slave.* New York: Johnson Reprint, 1970.

———. *The Negro in the American Rebellion.* Miami, Fla.: Mnemosyne Publishing, 1969.

Buckmaster, Henrietta. *Let My People Go: The Story of the Underground Railroad and the Growth of the Abolition Movement.* Reprinted from the 1941 edition. Columbia, S.C.: University of South Carolina Press, 1992.

Butler, Pierce. *Judah P. Benjamin.* Philadelphia: George W. Jacobs, 1907.

Cable, Mary. *Black Odyssey: The Case of the Slave Ship Amistad*. New York: Penguin Books, 1977.

"Child, Lydia Maria Francis" by Catherine Teets-Parzynski. *American National Biography*, IV, 806–808. New York: Oxford University Press, 1999.

———. *The Freedmen's Book*. Boston: Ticknor and Fields, 1865.

Coffin, Levi. *Reminiscences*. Cincinnati: Western Tract Society, 1876.

Conneau, Theophilus. *A Slaver's Log Book or 20 Years' Residence in Africa*. Englewood Cliffs, N.J.: Prentice-Hall, 1976.

Craton, Michael. *A History of the Bahamas*. Waterloo, Ontario: San Salvador Press, 1986.

Dictionary of Louisiana Biography, Glenn R. Conrad, general ed. Lafayette, La.: Louisiana Historical Association, 1988.

Douglass, Frederick. *Frederick Douglass Papers*, ed. by John W. Blassingame. New Haven: Yale University Press, 1979–1992.

———. "The Heroic Slave," in Julia Griffiths, ed. *Autographs for Freedom*. Boston: John R. Jewett, 1853. Reprinted in George Hendrick and Willene Hendrick, eds. *Two Slave Rebellions at Sea*. St. James, N.Y.: Brandywine Press, 2000.

———. *Life and Times*, facsimile of the 1881 edition. Secaucus, N.J.: Citadel Press, 1983.

———. *The Narrative and Selected Writings*, ed. by Michael Meyer. New York: Modern Library, 1984.

Equiano, Olaudah. *The Life of Olaudah Equiano* in *The Classic Slave Narratives*, ed. by Henry Louis Gates, Jr. New York: Mentor, 1987.

Evans, Eli N. *Judah P. Benjamin: The Jewish Confederate*. New York: Free Press, 1988.

Franklin, John Hope, and Alfred A. Moss, Jr. *From Slavery to Freedom*, 6th ed. New York: McGraw-Hill, 1988.

——— and Loren Schweninger. *Runaway Slaves: Rebels on the Plantation*. New York: Oxford University Press, 1999.

"Freeman, Theophilus." *Dictionary of Louisiana Biography*. Lafayette, La.: Louisiana Historical Association, 1988.

Gara, Larry. *The Liberty Line: The Legend of the Underground Rail-road*. Lexington: University of Kentucky Press, 1967.

Gates, Henry Louis, Jr., and Nellie Y. McKay, eds. *The Norton Anthology of African American Literature*. New York: W. W. Norton, 1997.

Gruesser, John Cullen. "Taking Liberties: Pauline Hopkins' Recasting of the Creole Rebellion," in *The Unruly Voice: Rediscovering Pauline Elizabeth Hopkins*, ed. by John Cullen Gruesser. Urbana: University of Illinois Press, 1996.

Harms, Robert. *The Diligent: A Voyage Through the Worlds of the Slave Trade*. New York: Basic Books, 2002.

Hill, Pascoe G. *Fifty Days on Board a Slave-Vessel*, first published in 1848. Baltimore: Black Classics Press, 1993.

Hill, Patricia Liggins, general ed. *Call & Response: The Riverside Anthology of the African American Literary Tradition*. Boston: Houghton Mifflin, 1998.

Jacobs, Harriet A. *Incidents in the Life of a Slave Girl*, and John S. Jacobs, *A True Tale of Slavery*, ed. by George Hendrick and Willene Hendrick. St. James, N.Y.: Brandywine Press, 1999.

Jervey, Edward D., and C. Edward Huber. "The Creole Affair," *Journal of Negro History* 65 (1980): 196–211.

Johnson, Walter. *Soul by Soul: Life Inside the Antebellum Slave Market*. Cambridge, Mass.: Harvard University Press, 1999.

Jones, Howard. *Mutiny on the Amistad*. New York: Oxford University Press, 1987.

———. "The Peculiar Institution and National Honor: The Case of the *Creole* Slave Revolt." *Civil War History* 21 (March 1975): 28–56.

Katz, Jonathan. *Gay American History*. New York: Harper & Row, 1985.

Katz, William Loren. *Breaking the Chains: African-American Slave Resistance*. New York: Atheneum, 1990.

Kleinman, Joseph, and Eileen Kurtis-Kleinman. *Life on an African Slave Ship*. San Diego: Lucent Books, 2001.

The Liberator, June 10, 1842. Reprints the *Friend of Man* article on Madison Washington.

London *Times*, May 8, 1842.

Louisiana Annual Reports X (March 1845): 202–354. *Reports of Cases Argued and Determined in the Supreme Court of Louisiana and in the Superior Court of the Territory of Louisiana*. St. Paul: West Publishing Co., 1907–1913.

McFeely, William S. *Frederick Douglass*. New York: W. W. Norton, 1991.

McKay, Nellie Y. "Introduction." *The Unruly Voice: Rediscovering Pauline Elizabeth Hopkins*, ed. by John Cullen Gruesser. Urbana: University of Illinois Press, 1996.

Mannix, Daniel P., and Malcolm Cowley. *Black Cargoes: A History of the Atlantic Slave Trade, 1518–1865*. New York: Penguin Books, 1962.

Meade, Robert Douthat. *Judah P. Benjamin: Confederate Statesman*. New York: Oxford University Press, 1943.

Melville, Herman. *White-Jacket or The World in a Man-of-War*. Evanston and Chicago: Northwestern University Press, 1970.

Merck Manual. Rahway, N.J.: Merck & Co., 1950.

New Orleans Picayune, December 3, 1841.

Nichols, Charles H. *Black Men in Chains*. New York: Lawrence Hill, 1972.

Northup, Solomon. *Twelve Years a Slave*, ed. by Sue Eakin and Joseph Logsdon. Baton Rouge: Louisiana State University Press, 1968.

Parker, John P. *His Promised Land*, ed. by Stuart Seely Sprague. New York: W. W. Norton, 1996.

Peterson, Bernard L., Jr. *Early Black American Playwrights and Dramatic Writers*. New York: Greenwood Press, 1990.

———. "Theodore James Ward." *American National Biography* 22:650–652. New York: Oxford University Press, 1999.

Pinckney, Darryl. "Introduction" to Harriet Beecher Stowe's *Uncle Tom's Cabin*. New York: Signet Classic, 1998.

Richmond (Virginia) *Enquirer*, January 1, March 22, 1842.

Sale, Maggie Montesinos. *The Slumbering Volcano: American Slave*

Ship Revolts and the Production of Rebellious Masculinity. Durham: Duke University Press, 1997.

Senate Documents, 27th Congress, 2nd Session, No. 51.

Shakespeare, William. *The Riverside Shakespeare.* Boston: Houghton Mifflin, 1974.

Siebert, Wilbur H. *The Underground Railroad from Slavery to Freedom*, first published in 1898. New York: Russell & Russell, 1967.

Stepto, Robert B. "Storytelling in Early Afro-American Fiction: Frederick Douglass' 'The Heroic Slave.'" *Georgia Review* 36 (Summer 1982): 355–368.

Still, William. *The Underground Rail Road.* New York: Arno Press, 1968. Reprint of the 1872 edition.

Stowe, Harriet Beecher. *Uncle Tom's Cabin*, with an introduction by Darryl Pinckney. New York: Signet Classic, 1998.

Thomas, Hugh. *The Slave Trade: The Story of the Atlantic Slave Trade, 1440–1870.* New York: Simon & Schuster, 1997.

Two Slave Rebellions at Sea: "The Heroic Slave" by Frederick Douglass and "Benito Cereno" by Herman Melville, edited by George Hendrick and Willene Hendrick. St. James, N.Y.: Brandywine Press, 2000.

"Ward, Theodore." *Contemporary Authors* 125:476–477. Detroit: Gale Research, 1989.

Winks, Robin W. *The Blacks in Canada: A History*, 2nd ed. Montreal: McGill–Queen's University Press, 1997.

A Note on Sources

INTRODUCTION

For the official account of the mutiny on the *Creole*, we have used Senate Documents, 27 Cong., 2nd Sess., No. 51: "Message from the President of the United States." Cited hereinafter as Senate Documents, No. 51. This forty-six-page document, printed in 1842, contains correspondence about the *Creole* affair by Daniel Webster, U.S. secretary of state; John F. Bacon, U.S. consul in Nassau; Sir Francis Cockburn, governor general of the Bahamas; C. R. Nesbitt, colonial secretary in the Bahamas; and G. C. Anderson, attorney general in the Bahamas.

It also contains the testimony of William Woodside, master of the bark *Louisa*; William H. Merritt, slave guard on the *Creole*; Zephaniah C. Gifford, first mate on the *Creole*, who assumed command after the ship reached Nassau; Lucius Stevens, second mate on the *Creole*; Blinn Curtis, a sailor on the ship; Captain Ensor; Theophilus Mc-Cargo, young nephew of the slave trader who owned many of the slaves being shipped on the *Creole*; and Joseph Leitner, a Prussian serving as assistant steward in exchange for passage to New Orleans.

Also included in the document is a "Protest"—a written declaration swearing that damages and losses were sustained from unavoidable causes—sworn to by the officers and crew of the ship once it reached the Bahamas. We refer to it in the text as the Nassau Protest. In it the nineteen mutineers are specifically named.

All but five of the slaves left the ship in Nassau, and after a few days the *Creole* continued on to New Orleans. Once there, the officers and crew filed another Protest, which we refer to in the text as the New Orleans Protest. This protest may also be found in Senate Documents, No. 51.

Throughout this work we use information and testimony from Senate Documents, No. 51. We recognize that all the testimony by officers and crew of the *Creole*, U.S. consul Bacon, and Master Woodside was entirely pro-slavery. As far as we can determine, no testimony was taken from the slaves.

One other major source for information about the *Creole* mutiny may be found in *Louisiana Annual Reports* X (March 1845), documenting the lawsuits brought by slave owners against the insurance companies who were refusing to pay for the loss of the freed slaves on the *Creole*. This extensive document is referred to in the text as *Louisiana Annual Reports*. It includes materials from Senate Documents, No. 51, but also prints quotations from the ship's log, arguments of the attorneys, and cross-examination testimony.

Most of the details in Chapter One, "We Have Commenced," are scattered throughout Senate Documents, No. 51, but the information that male slaves were subject to being whipped if they went into the hold where women slaves were kept is found in *Louisiana Annual Reports*, p. 207.

The quotation from Robert Harms, *The Diligent: A Voyage Through the Worlds of the Slave Trade*, is on p. 410.

The quotation from Henry Highland Garnet's "An Address to the Slaves of the United States of America" is from *Call & Response*, p. 272.

We have used the excellent chronological account of the mutiny in Edward D. Jervey and C. Edward Huber, "The Creole Affair," *Journal of Negro History*, 65: 196–211.

I. "WE HAVE COMMENCED"

Information about the first minutes of the mutiny is taken from Senate Documents, No. 51 and *Louisiana Annual Reports*.

II. MADISON WASHINGTON: BEFORE THE MUTINY

For information about advertisements for runaway slaves, see John Hope Franklin and Loren Schweninger, *Runaway Slaves: Rebels on the Plantation*, pp. 209–210, 297–300, 330–331. The quotation about personality traits of runaway slaves is from p. 224.

The account of escape by sea is from Harriet Jacobs, *Incidents in the Life of a Slave Girl* and John S. Jacobs, *A True Tale of Slavery*, edited by Hendrick and Hendrick, pp. 119–125.

William Still in *The Underground Rail Road* gives the story of the runaways in the bateau, pp. 528–530.

The account of the escape of William and Ellen Craft is in Still's *The Underground Rail Road*, pp. 368–377. The slave trader's comments to "Gentleman" Craft are from Charles Nichols's *Black Men in Chains*, p. 255.

The account of John S. Jacobs's escape is from the Hendrick and Hendrick Introduction to *Incidents in the Life of a Slave Girl* and *A True Tale of Slavery*, p. ix.

The story of the escape of Henry "Box" Brown is from Still, *The Underground Rail Road*, pp. 81–86.

John Brown in *Slave Life in Georgia*, p. 81, describes the escape through the woods.

The story of the armed escapees who faced down the cowardly whites is from Still, *The Underground Rail Road*, pp.124–129.

Taper's letter is quoted in Franklin and Schweninger, *Runaway Slaves*, pp. 324–325. The quotation is reproduced as written.

Levi Coffin's *Reminiscences* offers one of the best accounts of the Underground Railroad. His quotes about conditions of escaped slaves in Canada and the number of blacks in Canada are on p. 253. Robin Winks in *The Blacks in Canada*, 2nd edition, discusses "How Many Negroes in Canada," pp. 484–496. It is extremely difficult to determine how many slaves settled in Canada. Winks discusses Hiram Wilson and black colonies in Canada. Our references are primarily to pp. 178–180. We found his Chapters 5, 6, and 7, pp. 114–232, extremely helpful for background information.

Winks discusses Josiah Henson on pp. 180–204, paying careful attention to the questionable identifications of Henson as the original for Stowe's Uncle Tom. We also use information about Henson from Darryl Pinckney's introduction to *Uncle Tom's Cabin*. The quote from Henson's autobiography is from that Introduction, p. xviii. Uncle Tom's words after he refused to be a runaway are from the Pinckney edition of that novel, p. 45.

The quote from Taper's letter is from Franklin and Schweninger, *Runaway Slaves*, pp. 324–325.

The account of Isaac Forman, distressed because his wife was still in bondage, is from Still, *The Underground Rail Road*, pp. 64–65.

The Department of Rare Books and Special Collections of the University of Rochester provided biographical information about Lindley Murray Moore and his wife.

The biographical information about Henry Highland Garnet is from Patricia Liggins Hill, ed., *Call & Response*, pp. 264–267. The quotation from Garnet's 1843 speech is from Hill, p. 272.

Quotations from Frederick Douglass's "Slavery, the Slumbering Volcano," with comments on Madison Washington, John Gurney, and Robert Purvis, are from the *Frederick Douglass Papers*, Series I, vol. II, 154–158.

The quotation from Coffin on the difficulty in raising money to buy the relatives of a slave is from his *Reminiscences*, p. 577.

Coffin's story about John White is in his *Reminiscences*, pp. 428–446. All quotations about Fairfield are from those pages.

Information about John P. Parker is from the Introduction to *His Promised Land*, p. 9. Parker's advice, "get another wife," is from p. 73.

The story of Jim, the cunning slave, is from Coffin's *Reminiscences*, pp. 139–144. All quotations about Jim are from those pages.

III. MADISON WASHINGTON'S CAPTURE AND SALE

All references to the *Friend of Man* article on Madison Washington are from the reprint in *The Liberator*, June 10, 1842, p. 1.

John Brown's account of the flogging of slaves is from his *Slave Life in Georgia*, pp. 97–98.

Walter Johnson in *Soul by Soul* has an excellent chapter, "Reading Bodies and Marking Race," pp. 135–161, with much information on how traders judged slaves. *Soul by Soul* is an extraordinary work of scholarship, and we are much indebted to it.

Theophilus Conneau's account of the examining of naked slaves is from *A Slaver's Log Book*, p. 71.

The Victorian version of the examination of slaves is quoted in Walter Johnson's *Soul by Soul*, p. 138. Johnson gives a more realistic account of the examinations on p. 141.

John Brown in *Slave Life in Georgia* describes the examination of slaves on p. 99.

Howard Jones writes about Cinqué's demonstration of his examination in *Mutiny on the Amistad*, p. 124.

The quote from John Brown's *Slave Life in Georgia* on slave women as concubines in Freeman's slave pen is on p. 95.

Walter Johnson on the indecent exams of slave women may be found in *Soul by Soul*, pp. 147–149.

John Brown on the chaos in the slave auction room is from his *Slave Life in Georgia*, p. 100.

Walter Johnson published parts of John White's account book in *Soul by Soul*, pp. 45–46.

The quotations from Daniel Hundley are also from *Soul by Soul*, pp. 24–25.

The description of the slave trader in *Uncle Tom's Cabin* is on p. 5 of the Pinckney edition of that novel.

Information about Goodin & Co., the slave pen managed and co-owned by Theophilus Freeman, and about Freeman himself, is from Brown, *Slave Life in Georgia*, pp. 88–100; Solomon Northup, *Twelve Years a Slave*, pp. 48–60; and Walter Johnson, *Soul by Soul*, *passim*. See also the Freeman entry in *Dictionary of Louisiana*, I, 323. Northup writes about his experiences in slave pens in Washington, D.C., and Richmond, Virginia, and on the *Orleans* on pp. 19–48. Sue Eakin and Joseph Logsdon in their introduction and notes to *Twelve Years a Slave* provide valuable background information.

The account of Freeman's plans to make the beautiful child Emily into a concubine is from Northup's *Twelve Years a Slave*, pp. 57–60. Johnson in *Soul by Soul* comments on Emily's plight on p. 152.

The description of a coffle is from Johnson's *Soul by Soul*, p. 60.

John Brown's description of the multiple rapes of a slave woman in a coffle is from *Slave Life in Georgia*, p. 19.

IV. THE SLAVE SHIPS

The quotation from de Zumara is from Hugh Thomas, *The Slave Trade*, pp. 21–22. Thomas's book is an exhaustive and authoritative study, and we are indebted to his careful research. Also recommended is *Black Cargoes* by Daniel P. Mannix and Malcolm Cowley. *Life on an African Slave Ship* is a good introduction to a complex subject; the authors, Joseph Kleinman and Eileen Kurtis-Kleinman, also chose excellent illustrations. Robert Harms's *The Diligent: A Voyage Through the Worlds of the Slave Trade* is highly recommended.

The quotations from John Newton about having absolute control on his vessel and on the brutalizing effects of the slave trade are from Kleinman and Kurtis-Kleinman, *Life on an African Slave Ship*, p. 19.

Thomas discusses the number of insurrections in *The Slave Trade*, p. 424. He quotes Newton about the treatment of slaves by seamen on p. 311.

The cursing and profane language of sailors is well known. Kleinman and Kurtis-Kleinman in *Life on an African Slave Ship* summarize the subject on p. 55.

Thomas on the examination of penises is from *The Slave Trade*, p. 433.

The discussion of death rates of slaves being transported to the Americas is from Mannix and Cowley, *Black Cargoes*, pp. 123–124.

The overnight death of fifty-four slaves is detailed in Pascoe Hill's *Fifty Days on Board a Slave-Vessel*, pp. 23–24. Hill describes the flogging on pp. 33–34.

Thomas in *The Slave Trade* discusses the mutiny on the *Kentucky* on pp. 718–719.

The account of the execution of slaves who revolted on the *Tryal* is from *Two Slave Rebellions at Sea*, edited by George Hendrick and Willene Hendrick, pp. 134–135.

Thomas in *The Slave Trade* writes of black slave women urging male slaves to attack the crew on p. 416; on slave ships as "half bedlam and half brothel" on p. 418; on the sadistic attack on a slave woman on p. 418; on the custom on an English slave ship for each sailor to have a "wife," p. 408; on John Newton's punishment of a sailor who seduced a slave, p. 408.

Equiano's quotations about the clerks' attacks "on the chastity of female slaves" and the sexual attacks on girls less than ten are from his *Life*, p. 74.

The quotation from John S. Jacobs is from *Incidents in the Life of a Slave Girl* by Harriet A. Jacobs and *A True Tale of Slavery* by John S. Jacobs, edited by Hendrick and Hendrick, p. 165.

The quotation from Herman Melville's *White-Jacket* is on pp. 375–376.

The quotation from John Brown on vice in the New Orleans slave pen is from *Slave Life in Georgia*, p. 95.

Thomas in *The Slave Trade*, pp. 551–552, discusses the ban on the importation of slaves into the United States. Howard Jones in *Mutiny on the Amistad*, pp. 16–17, discusses the ban on the introduction of slaves from Africa into Cuba.

The comments on conditions on the *Amistad* are from Jones's *Mutiny on the Amistad*, pp. 24, 44, 124. Celestino's threat to kill the Africans and salt their flesh is on p. 24.

The quotation from Captain Delano on the cruelty to captured slave mutineers on the *Tryal* is from his chapter on the mutiny in his *A Narrative of Voyages and Travels . . .* , reprinted in *Two Slave Rebellions at Sea*, pp. 120–121.

Northup's characterizations of his fellow slaves being shipped to New Orleans are from his *Twelve Years a Slave*, pp. 28–32, 33–40, 41–42.

Northup's accounts of life aboard the *Orleans* are from *Twelve Years a Slave*, pp. 42–43. His account of the planning of the mutiny and its failure are on pp. 43–46. Johnson calls Northup "a deeply prejudiced person" in *Soul by Soul*, p. 66.

Various editions of the *Merck Manual* give slightly different incubation periods for smallpox. We have used the 8th edition, 1950, pp. 677–684. The information in that edition was extensive since the disease was still found in various parts of the world at the time. After the eradication of smallpox, the *Merck Manual* reduced the amount of information it offered about the disease.

V. THE MUTINY ON THE *CREOLE*

Much of the information in this chapter is taken from Senate Documents, No. 51, and from *Louisiana Annual Reports* X. For the chronology of events during the mutiny and afterward, we have used "The Creole Affair" by Jervey and Huber.

All references to the log of the *Creole* are from *Louisiana Annual Reports* X, 339–340.

The confused accounts of the number of slaves on the *Creole* are from the ship's log and from the New Orleans Protest, in Senate Documents, No. 51, p. 37.

We quote Franklin and Schweninger, *Runaway Slaves*, p. 183, on free people of color who were forced back into slavery. For more information on this subject, see the chapter "Backward into Bondage" in *Runaway Slaves*, pp. 182–208.

The quotation about Captain Mary is from Harms, *The Diligent*, p. 318.

Walter Johnson in *Soul by Soul*, p. 63, speculates that slave women brought into the cabin as maids may have served the white men on the *Creole* as concubines. Johnson on p. 62 notes that separating slaves by sex not only was a deterrent to the spreading of sexually transmitted diseases but also helped prevent "starting a pregnancy."

Gifford's testimony about not searching the slaves for weapons is from *Louisiana Annual Reports* X, 217–218.

The account of the killing of the captain's dog is from the *New Orleans Picayune*, December 3, 1841, p. 2.

The comments about the mutineers keeping order over blacks and whites after the *Creole* had been seized are from *Louisiana Annual Reports* X, 209.

Leitner's comments about giving food and drink to the mutineers are from Senate Documents, No. 51, p. 27.

The slave owners wanted as few slaves as possible implicated in the mutiny. We are following the suggestion of Maggie Montesinos Sale, *The Slumbering Volcano: American Slave Ship Revolts and the Production of Rebellious Masculinity*, p. 123. Sale's two chapters on the *Creole* case, pp. 120–145 and 173–197, are carefully argued.

The report that one of the mutineers had picked out a wife from among the six maids is from the New Orleans Protest in Senate Documents, No. 51, p. 41; Dr. Ruffin's forcing Merritt not to write on the slate is from the same page.

Elijah Morris's statement that some slaves wanted to throw Stevens overboard is from Senate Documents, No. 51, p. 33.

Gifford's request to the quarantine officer that slaves have no communication with those on shore is from *Louisiana Annual Reports* X, 210.

VI.THE *CREOLE* SLAVES IN NASSAU

Most of the materials in this chapter are drawn from Senate Documents, No. 51, and *Louisiana Annual Reports* X.

Bacon's negotiations with Sir Francis Cockburn are detailed in Senate Documents, No. 51, pp. 2–10.

Sale in *The Slumbering Volcano*, p.123, discusses the wishes of the officers on the *Creole* to implicate as few slaves as possible as mutineers. We have found Sale's Chapter 3 on the *Creole* affair, pp. 120–145, useful.

Captain Fitzgerald's comment to Mary that the whites on the *Creole* should have been thrown overboard is from Senate Documents,

No. 51, p. 42. The same incident is reported in *Louisiana Annual Reports* X, 215.

The speculation on the number of blacks and whites in Nassau is from Senate Documents, No. 51, p. 42.

Reaction of the citizens of Nassau to whites on the *Creole*—they were called "pirates and slavers"—is from *Louisiana Annual Reports* X, 213.

Jervey and Huber in "The Creole Affair" are particularly good on the plan of Gifford and Bacon to retake the *Creole*, pp. 202–203.

Gifford's statement that the "musquito" fleet was acting on British instructions is reported in *Louisiana Annual Reports* X, 211.

Attorney General Anderson's actions on the *Creole* are reported in Senate Documents, No. 51, p. 43.

The account of slaves stealing money and clothes is from *Louisiana Annual Reports* X, 212.

Anderson's statement about the abolition of slavery is from *Louisiana Annual Reports* X, 251.

Gifford's statements that some freed slaves in Nassau wished to go on to New Orleans or were frightened and did not know what to do is from *Louisiana Annual Reports* X, 216–217.

Jervey and Huber in "The Creole Affair" provide information about the British judicial treatment of the mutineers in a Nassau jail, pp. 205–206.

The statement that the mutineers did what they did to gain their freedom is from Senate Documents, No. 51, p. 41.

John Cullen Gruesser in *The Unruly Voice*, p. 114, quotes William Wells Brown's sentence about Madison Washington remaining in Nassau.

VII. THE ENSUING CONTROVERSIES

The quotation from the *New Orleans Bulletin* is cited in Jervey and Huber, "The Creole Affair," p. 205.

The quotation from the *Charleston Mercury* is cited in Sale's

The Slumbering Volcano, p. 132. In her research Sale used many nineteenth-century newspapers. We are indebted to her careful work.

The quotation from the *New York Herald* was reprinted in the *Richmond Enquirer*, March 22, 1842.

William Ellery Channing's letter is cited in Jervey and Huber, "The Creole Affair," p. 205.

The quotations from Senators Calhoun and Preston are from Sale, *The Slumbering Volcano*, p. 130.

The quotation from Daniel Webster's instructions to Edward Everett is from Sale, *The Slumbering Volcano*, p. 131. Additional information about Webster and his position on the *Creole* case is from Jervey and Huber, "The Creole Affair," p. 206.

Frederick Douglass's comments on Webster are quoted from the introduction to *Two Slave Rebellions at Sea*, edited by Hendrick and Hendrick, p. 6.

Whittier's "Ichabod" was first printed in *Songs of Labor and Other Poems* (1850). The lines quoted here are from Nina Baym, general ed., *The Norton Anthology of American Literature*, I, 1461–1462.

For an excellent account of the Webster-Ashburton negotiations and the *Creole* affair, see Howard Jones, "The Peculiar Institution and National Honor: The Case of the *Creole* Slave Revolt," *Civil War History* 21 (March 1975): 28–50. Jervey and Huber in "The Creole Affair," p. 207, also give useful information. The *Spy* quotation is from the Jones article, p. 37.

Biographical information about Judah P. Benjamin is from Pierce Butler's *Judah P. Benjamin*, Robert D. Meade's *Judah P. Benjamin: Confederate Statesman*, and Eli N. Evans's *Judah P. Benjamin: The Jewish Confederate*.

Benjamin's quotations about the *Creole* not being seaworthy, not being properly policed, being overcrowded, and the slaves' natural desire for freedom are from *Louisiana Annual Reports* X, 259–261.

Robert D. Meade in *Judah P. Benjamin*, p. 41, quotes Benjamin's "What Is a Slave?" speech given at an insurance trial.

The "I Am a Jew" passage is from *The Merchant of Venice*, III. i. 58–67.

The award of $110,330 for slave "property" lost in Nassau is from Jervey and Huber, "The Creole Affair," p. 208.

APPENDIX: MADISON WASHINGTON AND FIVE WRITERS

Biographical information about Frederick Douglass is taken from Gates and McKay, eds., *The Norton Anthology of African American Literature*, pp. 299–302; Patricia Liggins Hill, ed., *Call & Response*, pp. 272–275; William S. McFeely, *Frederick Douglass*; and Douglass's own autobiographies. The quotations from "The Heroic Slave" are from the text reproduced in Hendrick and Hendrick, eds., *Two Slave Rebellions at Sea*, pp. 21–51. Two valuable articles are William L. Andrews, "The Novelization of Voice in Early African American Narrative," *PMLA* 105 (January 1990): 23–34, and Robert B. Stepto, "Storytelling in Early Afro-American Fiction: Frederick Douglass' 'The Heroic Slave,'" *Georgia Review* 36 (Summer 1982): 355–368. Stepto makes a case for the artistry of "The Heroic Slave." See also "A Comparative Exploration of Narrative Ambiguities in Frederick Douglass' Two Versions of *The Heroic Slave* (1853–1863?)" by Celeste-Marie Bernier, in *Slavery and Abolition* 22 (August 2001): 69–86.

Biographical information about William Wells Brown is from Gates and McKay, eds., *The Norton Anthology of African American Literature*, pp. 245–247; Patricia Liggins Hill, ed., *Call & Response*, pp. 513–515; and Brown's *Narrative of William W. Brown, a Fugitive Slave*. Quotations from "Slave Revolt at Sea" are from Brown, *The Negro in the American Rebellion*, pp. 26–36.

Biographical information about Lydia Maria Child is from the sketch of her in *American National Biography* IV:806–808. Quotations from "Madison Washington" are from *The Freedmen's Book*, pp. 147–154. The quotation from her introduction ("To the Freedmen") to that book is on an unnumbered page.

Biographical information about Pauline Elizabeth Hopkins is from Gates and McKay, eds., *The Norton Anthology of African American Literature*, pp. 569–570, and John Cullen Gruesser, *The Unruly*

Voice: Rediscovering Pauline Elizabeth Hopkins, especially the "Introduction" by Nellie Y. McKay, pp. 1–20. Gruesser's "Taking Liberties: Pauline Hopkins' Recasting of the Creole Rebellion" is in *The Unruly Voice*, pp. 98–118; Gruesser discusses the change of name from Washington to Monroe on pp. 104–106. Quotations from "A Dash for Liberty" are from Elizabeth Ammons, ed., *Short Fiction by Black Women, 1900–1920*, pp. 89–98.

Biographical information about Theodore (Ted) Ward is from the entry on Ward in *Contemporary Authors* 125:476–477 and the Bernard L. Peterson, Jr., sketch of Ward in *American National Biography* 22:650–652. Peterson briefly describes many of Ward's dramas, including the unpublished and unproduced ones, in *Early Black American Playwrights and Dramatic Writers*. We have read, but have not quoted from, the typescript of *Madison* in the Hatch-Billops Collection in New York City.

Index

A NOTE ON THE AUTHORS

George Hendrick and Willene Hendrick, independent scholars, live in Urbana, Illinois. Together they have published *On the Illinois Frontier: Dr. Hiram Rutherford, 1840–1848*; *Katherine Anne Porter*, revised edition; *The Savour of Salt: A Henry Salt Anthology*; *Ham Jones, Antebellum Southern Humorist: An Anthology*; Salt's *Life of Thoreau* (with Fritz Oehlschlaeger); Sandburg's *Billy Sunday and Other Poems*; *Selected Poems of Carl Sandburg*; Sandburg's *Poems for the People*; *Incidents in the Life of a Slave Girl and A True Tale of Slavery*; and *Two Slave Rebellions at Sea*.